NOT IN THE SCRIPT

NOT IN THE SCRIPT

Performance Monologues from Unexpected Places

Edited by
JOHN McCALLUM
and
JENNY NICHOLLS

CURRENCY PRESS
SYDNEY

First published in 2016
by Currency Press Pty Ltd,
PO Box 2287, Strawberry Hills, NSW, 2012, Australia
enquiries@currency.com.au
www.currency.com.au

Cataloguing-in-Publication data for this title is available from the National Library of Australia website: www.nla.gov.au.

Cover design Alissa Dinallo for Currency Press.
Internal design by Emma Vine for Currency Press.
Typeset by Emma Rose Smith for Currency Press.
Printed by Ligare Book Printers, Riverwood, NSW.

CONTENTS

INTRODUCTION

In any piece worth performing there is something happening underneath that is not in the script. As in life, people say things that they do not mean, for reasons that they do not fully understand. Or they say things that are profoundly influenced, or even contradicted, by the state of the world – the world of the performance or the world we actually live in.

The action of the piece is the audience's growing understanding of the interplay between what is and what is not in the script. It could be their gradual realisation that not all is as it seems, or sometimes their knowledge that the character is lying, deluded, concealing something from themselves, masking a deeper truth, or perhaps simply being mischievous. A good performer finds that underlying action and plays it, while at the same delivering the words and performing the activities. The audience picks up cues and clues that guide their expectations, which keep changing as the theatrical structure of the piece is developed.

In a monologue taken from a play or specially written for performance, this covert action is often a subtext, or a dramatic irony in which the audiences knows something that the character doesn't. The pieces collected here sometimes use subtext and irony, but more often they take their action from a gradually-revealed context. The questions that guide the audience's expectations, and therefore the action, are not 'What is this person telling me?' but 'Why are they telling me this?', 'What is it about the world that I know that makes me doubt what they are saying?' or simply 'What is really going on underneath this?' Sometimes we come to know the answers as we watch, and sometimes we don't, and continue to wonder. Often a revelation at the end will change our entire understanding of what we have been experiencing.

The other, more obvious, reason for the title of this anthology is that none of these pieces come from a play or a monologue written to be performed. They are taken from short stories, novels or memoirs, in which complex worlds can be created in ways that are different from the ways in which they are created in plays. Many novels explain everything, in a way that plays cannot and should not try to do. The narrative voice of a novel written in the third person can know much more than any of the characters ever can. Even in the case of a novel written in the first person, perhaps by an unreliable narrator, there will often be two or three hundred pages of context that is very hard to play on stage in the brief time allowed for a performance for an exam or an audition.

But it is worth the effort. These pieces are offered as provocations. The aim of this anthology is to encourage students and actors wanting interesting pieces to perform to look beyond the usual sources. The ones chosen here are sometimes challenging but they all have something interesting to play with.

There is some wonderful writing here. The language, whether formal or vernacular, is to be relished. You can have a lot of fun speaking the words of these great authors. You can also create characters who speak to someone – the audience or someone else imagined on the stage – for interesting reasons that will allow you to lead, tease and provoke the audience. In many of these pieces you will have to evoke, in the dialogue passages, several figures other than the speaker, but in all of them there is your character playing the voices. When you are performing dialogue with other characters it is always your character whose attitude inflects how the other people speak. You can convey a lot about your character by how he or she speaks what they are saying. You may need to add or delete words or phrases, once you have found the central character, to make the piece your own.

The people speaking here come from many different backgrounds of time period, class, gender and culture. There are men and women; there are characters from many different cultural backgrounds; and there are people speaking from a wide range of experiences – some terrible, some joyful, some sad, some cheerful – but all of them, we think, are in some way transformed, at least within the piece as you will be performing it. There is even one (Breq) who is an Artificial Intelligence disturbed by what it feels as the stirrings of a human conscience.

We encourage you to be sensitive to issues of identity. It is sometimes not appropriate to perform an identity other than your own. If you have a point to make, it needs to become part of the action you are performing. Some identities are masked and some not. A character's sexuality can 'come out' as the action develops, but their physical characteristics are obvious as soon as they walk onstage. A woman is a woman and a man is a man, when you look at them onstage, but sometimes gender distinctions can be blurred, as they are in some of these pieces, such as Cal's.

Apart from the material from fiction and memoirs we have also included a poem, one of the greatest ever written, 'Song of Solomon', and another, offered as a little gift at the end: a wonderful work by the Dalit writer Jyoti Lanjewar. It is short but worth having a go at performing.

Before each piece there is a brief introduction explaining the context and also what we think you might be able to do with it in performance, but if you take up any of these pieces we strongly encourage you to go back to the source, read it and take on board what underlies the piece while you are working on how to perform it. We have chosen specific passages to include here but in all of the books from which they come there is plenty of other good material to play. And there are plenty of other good books.

You just have to look for the first-person narratives, a speaker with her or his own voice. In the opening piece here by Miranda July, a distinctively individual voice is deflected, for emotional reasons, into the third person. So perhaps you can look for possible performance pieces in third-person narratives too.

You can edit these pieces to suit your own performance, adding phrases for clarity or cutting material that, as you work on them, might not seem to fit. For example, you might like to remove certain descriptive phrases or words like 'he said' or 'she said'. We hope that drama and theatre students, and actors, will find good material to work with here. For the purposes of public examination or audition there are no copyright concerns, but if you subsequently perform these pieces for a paying audience then you will need to get performance permission.

We have assumed that you may not have access to a lot of production resources and that you will be alone on stage, with perhaps some basic costumes, props and sound. For most of these pieces it will just be you and your audience, which is as it should be.

We have had a wonderful time reading these books and choosing the pieces. We would like to thank the many people who have pointed us towards great books that we hadn't read before, and especially those whose suggestions have ended up here: Stefania Cox, Deborah Franco, Claire Grady, George Mannix, Jessica McCallum, Miranda McCallum, Penny McCue, Robyn Philip, Emma Rose Smith, Christine Stevenson and Angela Voerman.

John McCallum and Jenny Nicholls
Sydney, 2016

THIS PERSON

From no one belongs here more than you
by Miranda July

This is a complete stand-alone text, with no context other than what you can glean from what is said in it. The speaker obviously means herself when she talks about 'this person' and there is a great deal of emotional subtext when you play it for this. In performance she would be talking to the audience about what is clearly at first a fantasy. You could prompt the audience every time she says 'this person.'

In the happy first part of the text there are many hints about what 'this person' has been through, and in the second part there seems to be an underlying loneliness.

Maybe she is depressed, and so retreats to her bath to escape; or maybe she is being sensible, after having a fantasy that we can all understand (everyone she has ever known suddenly loving her). Maybe she settles happily into her bath because she simply wants to get on with her life. In performance it would be good to keep several possibilities open, in a state of theatrical tension. In any case, the journey is from the fantasy to the reality.

Someone is getting excited. Somebody somewhere is shaking with excitement because something tremendous is about to happen to this person. This person has dressed for the occasion. This person has hoped and dreamed and now it is really happening and this person can hardly believe it. But believing is not an issue here, the time for faith and fantasy is over, it is really really happening. Possibly there is some kneeling, such as when one is knighted. One is almost never knighted. But this person may kneel and receive a tap on each shoulder with a sword. Or, more likely, this person will be in a car or a store or under a vinyl canopy when it happens. Or online or on the phone. It could be an e-mail re: your knighthood. Or a long, laughing, rambling phone message in which every person this person has ever known is talking on a speakerphone and they are all saying, You have passed the test, it was all just a test, we were only kidding, real life is so much better than that. This person is laughing out loud with relief and playing the message back to get the address of the place where every person this person has ever known is waiting to hug this person and bring her into the fold of life. It is really exciting, and it's not just a dream, it's real.

They are all waiting by a picnic table in a park this person has driven past many times before. There they are, it's everyone. There are balloons taped to the benches, and the girl this person used to stand next to at the bus stop is waving a streamer. Everyone is smiling. For a moment this person is almost creeped out by the scene, but it would be so like this person to become depressed on the happiest day ever, and so this person bucks up and joins the crowd.

Teachers of subjects that this person wasn't even good at are kissing this person and renouncing the very subjects they taught. Math teachers are saying that math was just a funny way of saying 'I love you.' But now they are simply saying it, I love you, and the chemistry and PE teachers are also saying it and this person can tell they really mean it. It's totally amazing. Certain jerks and idiots and assholes appear from time to time, and it is as if they have had plastic surgery, their faces are disfigured with love. The handsome assholes are plain and kind, and the ugly jerks are sweet, and they are folding this person's sweater and putting it somewhere where it won't get dirty. Best of all, every person this person has ever loved is there. Even the ones who got away. They hold this person's hand and tell this person how hard it was to pretend to get mad and drive off and never come back. This person almost can't believe it, it seemed so real, this person's heart was broken and has healed and now this person hardly knows what to think. This person is almost mad. But everyone soothes this person. Everyone explains that it was absolutely necessary to know how strong this person was. Oh, look, there's the doctor who prescribed the medicine that made this person temporarily blind. And the man who paid this person two thousand dollars to have sex with him three times when this person was very broke. Both of these men are in attendance, they seem to know each other. They both have little medals that they are pinning on this person; they are badges of great honor and strength. The badges sparkle in the sunlight, and everyone cheers.

This person suddenly feels the need to check her post office box. It is an old habit, and even if everything is going to be terrific from now on, this person still wants mail. This person says she will be right back and everyone this person has ever known says, Fine, take your time. This person gets in her car and drives to the post office and opens the box and there is nothing. Even though it is a Tuesday, which is famously a good day for mail. This person is so disappointed, this person gets back in the car and, having completely forgotten about the picnic, drives home and checks the voice mail and there are no new messages, just the old one about 'passing the test' and 'life being better'. There are no e-mails, either, probably because everyone is at the picnic. This person can't seem to go back to the picnic. This person realizes that staying home means blowing off everyone this person has ever known. But the desire to stay in is very strong. This person wants to run a bath and then read in bed.

In the bathtub this person pushes the bubbles around and listens to the sound of millions of them popping at once. It almost makes one smooth sound instead of many tiny sounds. This person's breasts barely jut out of the water. This person pushes the bubbles onto the breasts and makes weird shapes with the foam. By now everyone must have realized that this person is not coming back to the picnic. Everyone was wrong; this person is not who they thought this person was. This person plunges underwater and moves her hair around like a sea anemone. This person can stay underwater for an impressively long time but only in a bathtub. This person wonders if there will ever be an Olympic contest for holding your breath under bathwater. If there were such a contest, this person would surely win it. An Olympic medal might redeem this person in the eyes of everyone this person has ever known. But no such contest exists, so there will be no redeeming. This person mourns the fact that she has ruined her one chance to be loved by everyone; as this person climbs into bed, the weight of this tragedy seems to bear down upon this person's chest. And it is a comforting weight, almost human in heft. This person sighs. This person's eyes begin to close, this person sleeps.

J.

From *Three Men in a Boat*

by Jerome K. Jerome

This is the opening passage from one of the great comic novels of the nineteenth century, first published in 1889. J. is accustomed to a good life of eating, drinking, larking about with his friends and not working more than he has to, but he is not an aristocrat. (If you are looking for a similar comic style from an endearing aristocratic twit you could try almost any of the P.G. Wodehouse novels about Bertie Wooster and his famous butler Jeeves.)

J.'s style, as you can see, is self-dramatising but also oddly innocent and ingenuous. You will have to decide the extent of his self-awareness. He is obviously claiming to believe all the information that he has found about his supposed illnesses, including the advertisements, but is he also conscious of the comic effect? He certainly shouldn't play it too much for laughs. The comedy depends on his (apparent) sincerity. There is something attractive about his cheerful acceptance of everything, especially at the end.

You could play on this old piece's obvious relevance in these times of scam 'complementary medicine' and hypochondriacal Google self-diagnosis.

There were four of us – George, and William Samuel Harris, and myself, and Montmorency. We were sitting in my room, smoking, and talking about how bad we were – bad from a medical point of view I mean, of course.

We were all feeling seedy, and we were getting quite nervous about it. Harris said he felt such extraordinary fits of giddiness come over him at times, that he hardly knew what he was doing; and then George said that *he* had fits of giddiness too, and hardly knew what *he* was doing. With me, it was my liver that was out of order. I knew it was my liver that was out of order, because I had just been reading a patent liver-pill circular, in which were detailed various symptoms by which a man could tell when his liver was out of order. I had them all.

It is a most extraordinary thing, but I never read a patent medicine advertisement without being impelled to the conclusion that I am suffering from the particular disease therein dealt with in its most virulent form. The diagnosis seems in every case to correspond exactly with all the sensations that I have ever felt.

I remember going to the British Museum one day to read up the treatment for some slight ailment of which I had a touch – hay fever, I fancy it was. I got down the book, and read all I came to read; and then, in an unthinking moment, I idly turned the leaves, and began to indolently study diseases, generally. I forget which was the first distemper I plunged into – some fearful, devastating scourge, I know – and, before I had glanced half down the list of 'premonitory symptoms', it was borne in upon me that I had fairly got it.

I sat for a while frozen with horror; and then in the listlessness of despair, I again turned over the pages. I came to typhoid fever – read the symptoms – discovered that I had typhoid fever, must have had it for months without knowing it – wondered what else I had got; turned up St Vitus's Dance – found, as I expected, that I had that too – began to get interested in my case, and determined to sift it to the bottom, and so started alphabetically – read up ague, and learnt that I was sickening for it, and that the acute stage would commence in about another fortnight. Bright's disease, I was relieved to find, I had only in a modified form, and, so far as that was concerned, I might live for years. Cholera I had, with severe complications; and diphtheria I seemed to have been born with. I plodded conscientiously through the twenty-six letters, and the only malady I could conclude I had not got was housemaid's knee.

I felt rather hurt about this at first; it seemed somehow to be a sort of slight. Why hadn't I got housemaid's knee? Why this invidious reservation? After a while, however, less grasping feelings prevailed. I reflected that I had every other known malady in the pharmacology, and I grew less selfish, and determined to do without housemaid's knee. Gout, in its most malignant stage, it would appear, had seized me without my being aware of it; and zymosis I had evidently been suffering with from boyhood. There were no more diseases after zymosis, so I concluded there was nothing else the matter with me.

I sat and pondered. I thought what an interesting case I must be from a medical point of view, what an acquisition I should be to a class! Students would have no need 'to walk the hospitals', if they had me. I was a hospital in myself. All they need do would be to walk around me, and, after that, take their diploma.

Then I wondered how long I had to live. I tried to examine myself. I felt my pulse. I could not at first feel any pulse at all. Then, all of a sudden, it seemed to start off. I pulled out my watch and timed it. I made it a hundred and forty-seven to the minute. I tried to feel my heart. I could not feel my heart. It had stopped beating. I have since been induced to come to the opinion that it must have been there all the time, and must have been beating, but I cannot account for it. I patted myself all over my front, from what I call my waist up to my head, and I went a bit round each side, and a little way up the back. But I could not feel or hear anything. I tried to look at my tongue. I stuck it out as far as ever it would go, and I shut one eye, and tried to examine it with the other. I could only see the tip, and the only thing that I could gain from that was to feel more certain than before that I had scarlet fever.

I had walked into that reading-room a happy healthy man. I crawled out a decrepit wreck.

I went to my medical man. He is an old chum of mine, and feels my pulse, and looks at my tongue, and talks about the weather, all for nothing, when I fancy I'm ill; so I thought I would do him a good turn by going to him now. 'What a doctor wants,' I said, 'is practice. He shall have me. He will get more practice out of me than out of seventeen hundred of your ordinary, commonplace patients, with only one or two diseases each.' So I went straight up and saw him, and he said:

'Well, what's the matter with you?'

I said:

'I will not take up your time, dear boy, with telling you what is the matter with me. Life is brief, and you might pass away before I had finished. But I will tell you what is *not* the matter with me. I have not got housemaid's knee. Why I have not got housemaid's knee, I cannot tell you;

but the fact remains that I have not got it. Everything else, however, I *have* got.'

And I told him how I came to discover it all.

Then he opened me and looked down me, and clutched hold of my wrist, and then he hit me over the chest when I wasn't expecting it – a cowardly thing to do, I call it – and immediately afterwards butted me with the side of his head. After that, he sat down and wrote out a prescription, and folded it up and gave it me, and I put it in my pocket and went out.

I did not open it. I took it to the nearest chemist's, and handed it in. The man read it, and then handed it back.

He said he didn't keep it.

I said:

'You are a chemist?'

He said:

'I am a chemist. If I was a co-operative stores and family hotel combined, I might be able to oblige you. Being only a chemist hampers me.'

I read the prescription. It ran:

1 lb beefsteak, with
1 pt bitter beer,
every 6 hours.
1 ten-mile walk every morning.
1 bed at 11 sharp every night.
And don't stuff up your head with things you don't understand.

I followed the directions, with the happy result – speaking for myself – that my life was preserved, and is still going on.

SUNNY

From *Purple Threads*

by Jeanine Leane

The narrator of this novel is a Wiradjuri woman from southern New South Wales, brought up by loving Aunties and her Nan. This story is a reminiscence from her youth, when she was six, and had only a fleeting understanding of what the events she now describes actually meant.

In performance the perspective is that of a child but we should be made to understand, as the young Sunny doesn't quite grasp, that the abused woman Milli has killed her husband, Alfi Schutz, after he returned during the storm in a violent drunken rage. The Aunties take control and rescue Milli and her children, and then go out to bury Alfi's body. Performing this you will have to play the Aunties and Nan, but also evoke Milli and her children, who are mostly silent presences.

The story here is full of human tenderness and also love for the land. Nature, gardens and the wildflowers of their home feature prominently. The storm that Sunny so vividly describes is a disruption in her young life, and the positive side of it is the rescue of Milli.

This is an edited version of a much longer chapter in the book.

One baking January, Alfi Schutz moved in to the old workers' hut on Cooper's farm, down the hill and across the road. Old man Cooper had survived the big drought of '64 by selling off all his stock, moving his family to town and sacking all his workers. The winter rains had been good the year before and promised to be good again this season, and while he had no intention of moving his missus and kids back to the homestead he had plans to revitalise the farm.

Old man Cooper hired Alfi Schutz to clear his land and shoot out all the kangaroos, stray dogs and feral animals. Aunty Boo said she heard from the Aunties in town that Alfi came out west to avoid some trouble in Sydney. He had a reputation as a deadly shot. He drove a battered old ute with meat hooks hung across the back bars. Pretty soon we saw the ugly evidence of his work. Carcasses of stray dogs, foxes and cats hung putrid and flyblown from Cooper's fences. Sometimes the stench of rotting flesh travelled all the way to our house on the hot afternoon wind.

'I'd like to hang that one on a barbed-wire fence by his hind leg,' Auntie Boo said as she stared out the window at Alfi's latest victims. 'Can't let the bloody dogs outta me sight now.'

'Must be some woman up there,' Nan said. 'Cleaned up the front o' the house real nice.'

'Liked it better when the whole bloody farm was empty,' Aunty Boo huffed.

That was the summer Milli and Annie came to us. [...]

We met Milli on the road that February. She was walking to town. Annie looked like a little monkey as she clung with her legs to the bump on Milli's stomach. Although summer's back was broken, the day was hot and dusty. Aunty Boo pulled over.

'Want a ride to town, darl?'

Milli tilted her hat forward and spoke to the ground. Annie buried her face in her mother's chest.

'Um, yes please, if it's no trouble.'

'Jump in front with the little fella.'

Aunty shot us a look that told us to move into the back. Milli climbed in the front.

'How old is the little one?' Auntie Boo asked as she pulled away.

'Not two yet, missus,' Milli spoke to the dashboard.

Aunty laughed. 'No "missus", babe. Jus' call me Boo.'

'I'm Milli,' she said to the floor. 'Baby's name is Annie.'

Despite our best efforts my sister and I couldn't coax Annie to play with us. She was shy and kept to her mother's chest. My attention turned to the dark ring around Milli's eye. My sister and I were no strangers to bruises on our legs and arms from all the trees we climbed, but we'd never seen a black eye before. [...]

Country oozed water that winter. It fell from the sky and rose from the ground. Water from the hills met swollen river flats and turned wheat plains to swamplands. Big floods washed away the farmers' profits and losses in one giant tongue of brown water.

'Gunna be wet one this year,' Nan said as she stepped back and looked with satisfaction at the roof-high pile of wood we'd made on the veranda.

By August the rain had really set in, steady at first but swelling with each day. One dark afternoon Aunty Boo picked us up early from school. The low-hanging clouds were bluish-black, like the bruises we saw on Milli's face.

'Won't stop fer weeks now, girls.' The old Ford crawled through sheets of water on the road. 'Come t'night, reckon the road'll be cut!'

Aunty Bubby had all the baby lambs under the kitchen stove; the sheep were taking refuge on hessian bags by the copper in the wash shed. Nan made us toast and jam and we settled in by the fire with the lambs. The rain was so heavy we didn't hear the jangle of Alfi's meat hooks when he set off for town that evening.

The driving rain broke into a wild storm. Thunder bounced between the peaks of the hills and made the plates on the dresser shake. My sister and I wriggled on Aunty Bubby's lap as she read to us. The dogs couldn't settle either. Nan paced the kitchen and said she felt a bit like the dogs. The storm howled. Ginger made low growling sounds and Gypsy's ears twitched and her fur stood on end.

When Aunty Boo checked the windows, she saw a dim torchlight making its way back to Cooper's hut. 'Must be him.' She jerked her head in the direction of the road. 'Musta got 'is truck bogged on the dirt road by the turn-off an' 'ad to walk home.'

The storm roared on. It was an uneasy night. We might have heard something had it not been for the rain on the roof. The thunder was so loud you couldn't have heard a cannon blast above it. The dogs woke us long before Milli made it to the veranda. Aunty Boo was standing right behind the door with her snake stick as Milli came into the light with the baby and Annie under her coat.

I said nothing about the blood on her hands and face. Come to think of it, no one did. Nan just grabbed the baby and Aunty Bubby prised Annie's little hands from her mother's skirt and handed her to Star and me before she rushed Milli off to the wash shed with a big steaming kettle of water.

Milli looked like a ghost when she came back wearing one of Nan's dresses. Nan tucked her up in her big bed with her sleeping babies and some tea and toast.

'Donchya worry none, Milli-girl,' Nan said.

But I heard Milli crying.

I was surprised to see Aunty Bubby and Aunty Boo walk back into the kitchen in their gumboots and raincoats. I wondered where they could be going so late, but I knew better than to ask.

Nan didn't ask either, just shook a gnarled finger. 'Youse girls be careful.'

The Aunties nodded, and Aunty Boo called, 'Come on, Gyp! Where are ya, Ginger?'

Gypsy and Ginger bounded to the door and Aunty Boo grabbed her snake stick from the corner and flung the front door open. I saw the wheelbarrow and shovel outside. The women disappeared into the storm.

[...]

I loved it when it rained this way. Come to think of it, we all did. We were on high ground. The road below us crossed the creek and the river three times between home and Gundagai. Sometimes we were cut off by the rising water for weeks in winter. The phone lines often went down too. It meant no school. It meant days at home with the Aunties and Nan and all their wet weather stories and games.

Even Milli laughed sometimes as the days passed. Annie let us read to her by the fire. The baby learnt to smile.

The creek between our place and Cooper's rose higher and higher. Near Gundagai the Murrumbidgee broke its banks. Centuries-old eucalyptus on the river flats fell like skittles as the huge snake of water flooded the land. And just as Nan predicted, the workers' hut on the creek flats washed away.

One night I heard Milli crying.

'Donchya worry, Milli-girl,' Nan soothed. 'Time this flood's done be a lot of things washed away an' gone f'rever, jus' you wait an' see. River's a powerful thing, jus' swallows up some things an' prob'ly for the betta.'

'That's right, sista-girl,' Aunty Boo said. 'Donchya worry, Aunties'll look afta ya.'

CHARLIE

From *Jasper Jones* by Craig Silvey

Charlie is much younger than the events he is describing might suggest – he is about fourteen. He is innocent and a bit of a book nerd, whereas Jasper, whom he has known about town but only just met that night, is older, maybe fifteen, and wilder. In the novel we already know the events that are here revealed gradually through hints.

Charlie has been woken by Jasper in the middle of the night to come and help him with a terrible situation – his discovery of the hanged body of a local girl in his secret hiding place in the bush. Jasper is an outcast in their small town, with a drunken father, and there is no way he won't be blamed for her death, although he had nothing to do with it.

Underlying this piece is Charlie's horror at what he has just taken part in – the hiding of the body. In this extract this is only revealed at the end, but we should feel from the beginning the fear that he feels. As the piece develops we also come to understand the courage that he finds in himself, and the new-found loyalty he feels towards Jasper.

Suddenly Jasper Jones is up and lurching, huddled over like he's been shot in the stomach. Before I can panic, he starts evicting that noxious liquid in a thick sheet that seems almost to glow. He grips the empty bottle. It smells sour, his sick. It's bursting out of him. He locks up violently, like he's being held and punched in the stomach by invisible assailants. Jasper retches and coughs, breathing heavily on his haunches. He spits and groans softly before retching again. Then he finally stands up straight.

'I thought you said you could hold your liquor?' I ask.

Jasper spits again, wipes his mouth and smiles. 'Yeah, I can. Just not for long.'

He turns and stumblesteps towards the dam. Kneeling, he fills the bottle with water. He looks precarious. And he collapses back against the tree before he can drink any. The bottle spills. He's out to it. Oblivious and gone. Maybe that's all he wanted.

I notice it suddenly seems lighter in this space. First I wonder if I've just grown accustomed to the dark, if I've adapted. Then I shoot from my feet like a firecracker and shake him awake.

'Jasper, *shit*! It's almost dawn! We have to go back. Now! If my parents know I've been out, I am right in it!'

Jasper Jones squints and slowly glances up.

'What?' He seems to ponder it. 'Yeah, you're right. Okay, Charlie. Juss a second.'

His words are slurred. Now I really fear getting lost on our return. But not nearly as much as I fear my parents finding my bed empty. I can't even imagine.

'No, we have to go now!'

Jasper stands unsteadily and treads heavily. He slaps a hand on my shoulder. Looks at me, intent yet vacant. Full of sorrow. His breath is like acid.

'Orright. Less go.'

He pauses. And swaying slightly, he lingers and looks up at the ghostly eucalypt. In spite of my worried hurry, I don't rush him. He takes it in one last time before we turn to go.

The walk back feels much faster than when we first set out. Perhaps it's because I'm aware of where we're headed, or because I am almost treading on Jasper's achilles in my haste.

His shoulders have fallen forward slightly. He doesn't walk with that straight-backed poise or intensity he had earlier. He shakes his pack of cigarettes. Empty. So he shoves his hands into his pockets. We walk silently and quickly. Overhead, magpies stir and warble their morning song. The sun is coming like a harbinger of doom. Strangely, the easier it is to see and navigate, the more afraid and apprehensive I am. But at the least the night is over. There's some relief in that. I don't have to bury anybody else. I can sleep soon. Maybe. For a couple of hours at least.

We track back onto the narrow path. And when we walk along it, I feel a weird sense of kinship, like we're old friends. It's not without its share of comfort. I know where we are. There is nothing but familiarity in front of me. It's the same when we push through the bush and onto the road. It's as though I've been away a long time, and I've finally arrived home. With a horrible secret that I've got to cauterise and keep down.

The light is grey and grim, but strengthening quickly. We might make it before the world wakes. We just might.

Now I walk side by side with Jasper Jones. I ponder whether or not we should split up, whether it's dangerous to be seen together. Or, more to the point, I understand that if I'm seen with Jasper Jones, it might arouse suspicion. I breathe in quick, about to broach it, but I check myself. I suddenly don't wish to. And it's not a question of bravery. I don't know. It seems that because we've ridden through something serious and substantial, I feel a real sense of loyalty. I feel as though if we were to separate here it would sully some kind of tacit pact. We're comrades in some private war. Suddenly it feels important to stay together, side by side.

And so as we reach the sepia centre of Corrigan: the Miners' Hall, the Sovereign Hotel, the newly refurbished post office, then the crouching loom of the police station, I realise I am in this. Right in it. To whatever end. Of course, I'm afraid. But, walking in his shadow, I'm also buffeted by a sort of anticipation. Me and Jasper Jones, sleuths and partners. Thick as thieves. In spite of everything, it excites me a little to know I'll certainly be seeing him again. That he needs my help. I don't feel so ridiculous walking next to him anymore. I don't feel like an incongruous sidekick. While the rest of this town looks at Jasper Jones like he's no good, it thrills me that he treats me like I'm equal.

As we turn, finally, into my street and we stride quickly before broad frontyards, skirting the side of my house, I'm afforded some slim relief. It seems my parents are yet to stir. I haven't been caught by anybody. Yet. I don't imagine I'll hold this sense of fortune for long. Tonight's events still lurk in me cold and uneasy. Anchored in and stuck, like that poor girl we tethered to a stone. When I'm less stunned and tired, it's going to hurt. It's going to bubble up and burst in me, I know it.

It is dawn. It is light. But it still feels like the night.

I turn to Jasper. He looks exhausted. And it occurs to me that there is no break in this for him, there's no comfort, nowhere he can go and lie down and be looked after. Not anymore. If he had anywhere in this world, it's the place we've just come from; the place that has just broken his heart and put him at risk. He's right: shit has been taken from him his whole life.

He looks done in and drunk, but he arches his back with a jolt, projecting that toughness again.

I wonder where he's going to go now. If he's going to go sit someplace quiet and wait for the riot, or if he's going to go home, if that's what you would call it.

It makes me feel rotten for what I have. For what I've always had. I feel stupid and petty for ever having complained about anything. I feel like a spoiled little bastard, about to crawl into my safe nest, while Jasper Jones shoulders his burden alone. It isn't fair. It isn't fair at all. I want to invite Jasper in, give him my bed, and I hate myself because I can't and I won't. I feel sick that I'm going to wake up and have my breakfast made. That my mum is still alive and my dad is a kindly teetotaller. It isn't right. It just isn't right that I have so many things that he doesn't. I might blub again, but I reckon I'm too tired even to do that. I'm so overdone and overwhelmed.

I wipe my forehead. I was right; my relief was short.

Jasper Jones gives a weak, quick grin and claps my arm. He pockets his hands. We don't say a word. We just look and nod and shift our feet. There's nothing to say.

I shuck off my pansy sandals, move quietly up to the window. I hoist myself up and hold, like I'm on a pommel horse, but I'm stuck. I turn my head and hiss: 'Gissa hand?'

And Jasper strides over and hefts me easily. I'm through. I made it. Back on my bed.

'Thanks,' I whisper through the window.

'Yeah, same to you,' he says. 'I'll see you, Charlie.' He lingers, as though he has more to say, but just offers a brief wave.

And he's gone.

I slot the glass plates back in. It feels like I've broken into my own room. It doesn't feel like the same place I left. It doesn't feel like home, but it feels safe. I can feel the heat of the day threatening already, and the light is still blue-hued. I notice how dirty I am, how sweaty and scratched, how urgently my heart bangs at my ribs. Laura Wishart is gone. She really is. She was killed, in a strange clearing known only to Jasper Jones. And I saw her, hanging by a thread. Already dead. I helped carry her to a waterhole and I dropped her down and she sank with a stone. That's irrefutable. That's truth. That's what we know. I'm thirsty. I'm in trouble. I feel sick and I can't still this tremor. For some reason, I just know that if I'm in Jasper Jones' corner, it's going to be okay. That there's some kind of protection and rightness at work. I lie down. And it's over, for now.

MISS SMILLA

From *Miss Smilla's Feeling for Snow* by Peter Høeg

Miss Smilla is a young professional woman in Denmark, an outsider because of her Greenlander heritage. She is very smart and confident until she meets the neglected boy on the staircase, Isaiah. Julianne is Isaac's alcoholic mother.

Miss Smilla is telling this story to us because she wants to understand what the boy meant to her. He died not long after the meeting she describes. In the novel from which this extract is taken she embarks on an epic journey to find out more about him and why he died.

This piece opens with her at the funeral, then, after the third paragraph, switches into a flashback memory of her first meeting with him. There are three things at work in playing this part: her current grief as she tells the story, the crankiness of the encounter itself, and her growing amazement that he keeps coming back and seems to want so little. Try as she might to turn this child away, there is something about his lonely need for her – to the point of listening to her read out loud from an ancient geometry textbook – that strikes a deep chord in her. She seems to be both amazed and satisfied by her realisation in the final lines that she has made such a connection with him.

At Isaiah's funeral I thought that I must grieve. I spoke to the police officers and offered [his mother] Julianne a shoulder to lean on and took her over to a friend's place and came back, and the whole time I held the grief at bay with my left hand. Now it should be my turn to give in to sorrow.

But it's not yet time. Grief is a gift, something you have to earn. I have made myself a cup of peppermint tea and gone over to stand by the window. But nothing happens. Maybe because there's still one little thing I have to do, a single thing unfinished, the kind that can block a flow of emotions.

So I drink my tea while the traffic on Knippel's Bridge thins out, becoming separate red stripes of light in the night. Gradually a kind of peace comes over me. Finally it's enough that I can fall asleep.

It is a day in August a year and a half earlier that I meet Isaiah for the first time. A humid, leaden heat has transformed Copenhagen into an incubator for imminent madness. I have been sitting in a bus with that special pressure-cooker atmosphere, wearing a new dress of white linen, cut low in the back, trimmed with Valenciennes ruffles which took me a long time to steam-press so they'd stand up properly, and they have now wilted in the general depression.

There are those who head south this time of year. South to the heat. Personally, I've never been further than Koge, fifty kilometres south of Copenhagen. And don't plan to go either, until the nuclear winter has cooled down the whole continent.

It's the kind of day that might make you wonder about the meaning of life, and discover that there is none. And something is rooting around on the stairway, on the landing below my apartment.

When the first large shipments of Greenlanders began arriving in Denmark in the 1930s, one of the first things they wrote home was that Danes are such pigs: they keep dogs in their houses. For a moment I think it's a dog lying on the stairs. Then I see that it's a child, and this particular day that is not much better.

'Beat it, you little shit,' I say.

Isaiah looks up.

'*Peerit*,' he says. Beat it yourself.

There aren't many Danes who can tell by looking at me that I'm a Greenlander. They think there's a trace of something Asian, especially when I put a shadow under my cheekbones. But the boy on the stairs looks right at me with a gaze that cuts straight through to what he and I have in common. It's the kind of look you see in newborns. Later it vanishes, sometimes reappearing in extremely old people. This could be one reason I've never burdened my life with children – I've thought too much about why people lose the courage to look each other in the eye.

'Will you read me a story?'

I have a book in my hand. That's what's prompted his question.

One might say he looks like a forest elf. But since he is filthy, dressed only in underpants, and glistening with sweat, one might also say he looks like a seal pup.

'Piss off,' I say.

'Don't you like kids?'

'I eat kids.'

He steps aside.

'*Salluvutit*, you're lying,' he says as I go past.

At that moment I see two things in him that somehow link us together. I see that he is alone. The way someone in exile will always be. And I see that he is not afraid of solitude.

'What's the book?' he shouts after me.

'Euclid's *Elements*,' I say, slamming the door.

It turned out to be Euclid's *Elements*, after all.

That's the one I take out that very evening when the doorbell rings and he's standing outside, still in his underpants, staring straight at me; and I step aside and he walks into my apartment and into my life, never really to leave it again; then it is Euclid's *Elements* I take down from the bookshelf. As if to chase him away. As if to establish from the start that I have no books that can interest a child, that he and I cannot meet over a book, or in any other way. As if to avoid something.

We sit down on the sofa. He sits on the very edge, with his legs crossed, the way kids from Thule used to sit at Inglefield in the summertime, on the edge of the dog sleigh used as a bed inside the tent.

'"A point is that which cannot be divided. A line is a length without breadth."'

This book turns out to be the one he never comments on, and the one we keep returning to. Occasionally I try others. On one occasion I borrow the children's book *Rasmus Klump on the Ice Cap*. In all serenity he listens to the description of the first pictures. Then he points a finger at the picture of the bear Rasmus Klump.

'What does that one taste like?' he asks.

'"A semicircle is a figure contained within a diameter … and the circumference intersected by the diameter."'

For me, the reading goes through three phases on that first evening in August.

First there is simply irritation at the whole impractical situation. Then there is the state of mind that always comes over me at the mere thought of that book: veneration. The knowledge that it is the foundation, the boundary. That if you work your way backwards, past Lobachevsky and Newton and as far back as you can go, you end up with Euclid.

'"On the greater of two given unequal straight lines …"'

Then at some point I no longer see what I am reading. At some point there is only my voice in the living room and the light of the sunset from Sydhavnen. And then my voice isn't even there; it's just me and the boy. At some point I stop. And we simply sit there, gazing straight ahead, as if I were fifteen and he were sixteen, and we have reached 'the point of no return'. Some time later he gets up very quietly and leaves. I watch the sunset, which lasts three hours at this time of year. As if the sun, on the verge of leaving, had discovered qualities in the world that are now causing it to have second thoughts about departing.

Of course Euclid didn't scare him off. Of course it made no difference what I read. For that matter, I could have read aloud from the telephone directory. Or from Lewis and Carrisa's *Detection and Classification of Ice*. He would have come anyway, just to sit with me on the sofa.

During some periods he would come every day. And then a couple of weeks might pass when I would see him only once, and from a distance. But when he did come, it was usually just starting to get dark, when the day was over and Julianne was out cold.

Once in a while I would give him a bath. He didn't like hot water, but it was impossible to get him clean in cold. I would put him in the bath tub and turn on the hand-held shower. He wouldn't complain. Long ago he had learned to put up with such adversity. But not for one moment did he take his reproachful eyes off my face.

ELLIE

From *The Dead of the Night* by John Marsden

Ellie is an ordinary country girl, about eighteen years old. While she and her friends Fi, Robyn, Homer and Lee (her boyfriend) are camping in the bush, Australia is invaded and they return to find themselves caught up in a war. The book from which this piece comes is the second in a series that explores their adventures and their forced involvement in a major war.

Ellie is very good at guerilla fighting but deeply conflicted about the moral implications of what she and her friends are doing. She is speaking to the audience from hindsight, although the scene she is describing could be evoked in your performance.

There is a dying enemy soldier lying on the ground, wounded by Ellie with a rock to the head. As she speaks we should be aware of his presence, and of her friends around her. He had chased her friend Fi into the bush, apparently with the intention of raping her. Ellie is breathless, battered and bruised, and tired from a long flight from the enemy. She is dressed in ragged bush gear, with maybe a torn and worn T-shirt from her earlier, happier life. She probably looks at the body for a while before she speaks. Perhaps she has the little torch mentioned in the text. The subtext of the extract is her yearning for the simplicity of her life before the war, and the vulnerability that lies beneath the toughness she is being forced to adopt.

One of the things I find strangest and hardest [in this war] is that we're having such conversations. We should have been talking about discos and electronic mail and exams and bands. How could this have been happening to us? How could we have been huddled in the dark bush, cold and hungry and terrified, talking about who we should kill? We had no preparation for this, no background, no knowledge. We didn't know if we were doing the right thing, ever. We didn't know anything. We were just ordinary teenagers, so ordinary we were boring. Overnight they'd pulled the roof off our lives. And after they'd pulled off the roof they'd come in and torn down the curtains, ripped up the furniture, burnt the house and thrown us into the night, where we'd been forced to run and hide and live like wild animals. We had no foundations, and we had no secure walls around our lives any more. We were living in a strange long nightmare, where we had to make our own rules, invent new values, stumble around blindly, hoping we weren't making too many mistakes. We clung to what we knew and what we thought was right, but all the time those things too were being stripped from us. I didn't know if we'd be left with nothing, or if we'd be left with a new set of rules and attitudes and behaviours, so that we weren't able to recognise ourselves any more. We could end up as new, distorted, deformed creatures, with only a few physical resemblances to the people we once were.

Of course, in among all this we had moments – days sometimes – when we acted in ways that were 'normal', vaguely like the old days. But it was never the same. Even those moments were warped by what had happened to us, by the horrible new world that we'd been forced into. There seemed no end to it, no clues as to what we would become, nothing. Just day-to-day survival.

Homer had leaned over the young soldier on the ground and was going through his pockets. He gradually accumulated a little pile of items as we watched in silence. It was hard to see details in the dark, but there was a wallet and a knife and a couple of keys. Then, from a breast pocket, he pulled out a little torch, no bigger than a pen, and switched it on. In its light I saw just how badly hurt the soldier was. There was blood coming out of his ears and nose, and his scalp was matted with blood, so that the hairs of his head were wet and stuck together. I also saw how young he was. He could have been younger than us. His smooth skin looked as if no razor had ever touched it. I had to remind myself urgently, harshly, that he was a potential rapist, a potential killer. At the same time I knew I couldn't kill him.

[But we couldn't leave him there. His presence would betray our hideout.]

'We could move him a long way off,' said Robyn doubtfully, 'so that they wouldn't connect him with the tree and the cliff.'

'And if he wakes up?' I asked. 'We're not doctors. We don't know what might happen.'

'He'd at least have concussion,' Robyn said, even more doubtfully. 'He probably wouldn't remember where he was or what happened.'

No one bothered to point out all the flaws in the plan.

We sat there quietly watching. After about an hour I began to realise that the young soldier was going to solve the problem for us. I realised that his life was slowly ebbing away. He was dying on the ground in front of us, as we looked on without a word being spoken. We made no move to save him, though I doubt if we could have done much anyway. I felt sad. In the short time we'd been gathered around him I'd come to feel that I knew him, in a strange sort of way. Death seemed so personal, so close, when it came slowly, almost gently, like this. In touching him it touched us all. Every quarter hour or so Homer switched the torch on, but although it was still dark under the trees, we didn't really need it. I could see each rise and fall of the uniformed chest, could feel each struggle to draw the next breath. I began to hold my own breath as he finished exhaling, willing him to find more air. But gradually each breath became lighter, and the pause between each one longer. A feather resting on his mouth might have fluttered a little as he reached for another moment of life, but the feather would not have lifted at all.

It had been a cold night, and it was a cold morning, but for once I didn't feel it. Fi was huddled against me, her face turned away from the soldier, and she helped keep me warm. Every so often she shook, with a spasm that might have been caused by the cold. Robyn sat beside the soldier's head, watching him calmly. There was something beautiful about her face as she gazed at his. Homer sat behind his head, also watching calmly, but there was a dark shadow on his face and an impatience in the way he bent forward, like a cocked rifle. It made me nervous to see him like that.

There was a distant crack through the trees. I sat up a little and turned a little towards it. And then heard the shout.

'Ellie! Homer! Are you there?'

Wild relief ran through me.

'Lee! Over here!'

We heard his blundering footsteps then, running and crashing towards us. I stood and moved a few steps in his direction. He came clumsily through the tall trees, squeezing through a narrow gap right in front of me. I held out my arms and he grabbed me and hugged me, but all I could feel were the bones of his body. I didn't feel love or affection or warmth from him, just an ugly roughness, and relief perhaps. He pushed me away and looked around him. 'Anyone got any food? I'm starving.'

'No,' Robyn said, 'nothing.'

'We've got to get out of here,' Lee said. His eyes had passed over the soldier on the ground, but he hadn't shown any surprise. Now he focused on him. 'What's he doing here?'

'He followed Fi,' Homer said.

'He's still alive,' Lee said.

'Yes.'

'Well, what are you waiting for?'

I wasn't sure what he meant. 'We were waiting for you,' I said. 'And we didn't know what to do with him. But I think he's close to dying.'

'We've got to go,' Lee said again. His eyes scanned the ground. Suddenly he bent down and picked up the soldier's knife from the sad little pile of possessions. At first I thought he'd then overbalanced and fallen on the boy. I even gasped and started to say, 'Look out!' But I realised at once that it was deliberate. Lee had landed clumsily with his knees on the boy's chest and at the same time had buried the knife in him, aiming at the heart. The boy gave a terrible gasp and both his arms lifted slightly, with the fingers flailing. Homer switched on the torch and in its sharp focused light, like a scalpel, I saw the face go very white, and a rush of blood pour from the mouth as it slowly opened. It stayed open. Then something left the face, a spirit or something fled from it, and he was dead. His face became the colour of water, no colour at all.

[We dragged him away from the cliff and threw him into a gully and covered him with branches. Robyn] wrinkled her brow for a minute, then said, 'God, look after him.' Then after a pause she added in a strong voice, 'Amen.'

'Amen,' I said, and after a moment Lee said it too.

As we walked back to the others he said to Robyn, 'If you'd seen what I saw last night you wouldn't be praying for any of them. And you wouldn't be wondering if we've done the wrong thing. They're filth. They're vermin.'

I understood then why he'd pushed the knife into the soldier's chest, but I was still scared of him for having done it.

BREQ

From *Ancillary Justice*

by Ann Leckie

This is the opening scene of the first book in a trilogy of science fiction novels about an Artificial Intelligence (AI) – Breq – who is forced to download into a human body. The series is about, among many other things, Breq's gradual understanding of what it means to be, or to appear as, human. This scene should contain enough tension to play with these questions. After it, as the plot gets more and more complicated, it is hard to find an extract without too much backstory required, but we encourage you to read the book and try.

A person of any gender could play this scene. Breq's body is male (and so is that of Seivarden, the body she finds at the beginning) but it is technologically enhanced, and in any case gender is a fluid concept for an AI. As Breq explains, her native language uses 'she' to mark all genders.

In finding the right appearance and tone for this character you will have to weigh the importance of suggesting that she is not human against the importance of playing her irrationally human actions and feelings. In non-human mode she is very tough and rational, an AI on a mission. The mystery behind the scene is why she stops to help this apparently hopeless drug-addicted wreck. It is a question that she can't answer herself.

There's a kind of hard-boiled tone here. It's like Raymond Chandler's Philip Marlowe – a tough guy who walks the mean streets with a gun in his pocket and a heart of gold. (You can find many other passages with this style in Chandler's novels.)

Breq is addressing the audience but is highly conscious of Seivarden, whom she places, by her attention, somewhere in the space as she speaks to us.

The body lay naked and facedown, a deathly gray, spatters of blood staining the snow around it. It was minus fifteen degrees Celsius and a storm had passed just hours before. The snow stretched smooth in the wan sunrise, only a few tracks leading into a nearby ice-block building. A tavern. Or what passed for a tavern in this town.

There was something itchingly familiar about that out-thrown arm, the line from shoulder down to hip. But it was hardly possible I knew this person. I didn't know anyone here. This was the icy back end of a cold and isolated planet, as far from Radchaai ideas of civilisation as it was possible to be. I was only here, on this planet, in this town, because I had urgent business of my own. Bodies in the street were none of my concern.

Sometimes I don't know why I do the things I do. Even after all this time it's still a new thing for me not to know, not to have orders to follow from one moment to the next. So I can't explain to you why I stopped and with one foot lifted the naked shoulder so I could see the person's face.

Frozen, bruised, and bloody as she was, I knew her. Her name was Seivarden Vendaai, and a long time ago she had been one of my officers, a young lieutenant, eventually promoted to her own command, another ship. I had thought her a thousand years dead, but she was, undeniably, here. I crouched down and felt for a pulse, for the faintest stir of breath.

Still alive.

Seivarden Vendaai was no concern of mine anymore, wasn't my responsibility. And she had never been one of my favourite officers. I had obeyed her orders, of course, and she had never abused any ancillaries, never harmed any of my segments (as the occasional officer did). I had no reason to think badly of her. On the contrary, her manners were those of an educated, well-bred person of good family. Not toward me, of course – I wasn't a person, I was a piece of equipment, a part of the ship. But I had never particularly cared for her.

I rose and went into the tavern. The place was dark, the white of the ice walls long since covered over with grime or worse. The air smelled of alcohol and vomit. A barkeep stood behind a high bench. She was a native – short and fat, pale and wide-eyed. Three patrons sprawled in seats at a dirty table. Despite the cold they wore only trousers and quilted shirts – it was spring in this hemisphere of Nilt and they were enjoying the warm spell. They pretended not to see me, though they had certainly noticed me in the street and knew what motivated my entrance. Likely one or more of them had been involved; Seivarden hadn't been out there long, or she'd have been dead.

'I'll rent a sledge,' I said, 'and buy a hypothermia kit.'

Behind me one of the patrons chuckled and said, voice mocking, 'Aren't you a tough little girl.'

I turned to look at her, to study her face. She was taller than most Nilters, but fat and pale as any of them. She out-bulked me but I was taller, and I was also considerably stronger than I looked. She didn't realize what she was playing with. She was probably male, to judge from the angular maze-like patterns quilting her shirt. I wasn't entirely certain. It wouldn't have mattered, if I had been in Radch space. Radchaai don't care much about gender, and the language they speak – my own first language – doesn't mark gender in any way. This language we were speaking now did, and I could make trouble for myself if I used the wrong forms. It didn't help that cues meant to distinguish gender changed from place to place, sometimes radically, and rarely made much sense to me. [I was an Artifical Intelligence, once a ship, now downloaded into a human body.]

I decided to say nothing. After a couple of seconds she suddenly found something interesting in the tabletop. I could have killed her, right there, without much effort. I found the idea attractive. But right now Seivarden was my first priority. [...]

[I got her back to a room in town and patched her up.] A head injury and internal organ damage were the most dangerous possibilities. I broke open the two [medical] correctives I'd just bought and lifted the blanket to lay one across Seivarden's abdomen, watching it puddle and stretch and then harden into a clear shell. The other I held to the side of her face that seemed the most bruised. When that one had hardened, I took off my outer coat and lay down and slept.

Slightly more than seven and a half hours later, Seivarden stirred and I woke. 'Are you awake?' I asked. The corrective I'd applied held one eye closed, and one half of her mouth, but the bruising and swelling all over her face was much reduced. I considered for a moment what would be the right facial expression, and made it. 'I found you in the snow, in front of a tavern. You looked like you needed help.' She gave a faint rasp of breath but didn't turn her head toward me. 'Are you hungry?' No answer, just a vacant stare. 'Did you hit your head?'

'No,' she said, quiet, her face relaxed and slack.

'Are you hungry?'

'No.'

'When did you eat last?'

'I don't know.' Her voice was calm, without inflection.

I pulled her upright and propped her against the gray-green wall, gingerly, not wanting to cause more injury, wary of her slumping over. She stayed sitting, so I slowly spooned some bread-and-water mush into her mouth, working cautiously around the corrective. 'Swallow,' I said, and she did. I gave her half of what was in the bowl that way and then I ate the rest myself, and brought in another pan of snow.

She watched me put another half-loaf of hard bread in the pan, but said nothing, her face still placid. 'What's your name?' I asked. No answer.

She'd taken kef, I guessed. Most people will tell you that kef suppresses emotion, which it does, but that's not all it does. There was a time when I could have explained exactly what kef does, and how, but I'm not what I once was.

As far as I knew, people took kef so they could stop feeling something. Or because they believed that, emotions out of the way, supreme rationality would result, utter logic, true enlightenment. But it doesn't work that way.

Pulling Seivarden out of the snow had cost me time and money that I could ill afford, and for what? Left to her own devices she would find herself another hit or three of kef, and she would find her way into another place like that grimy tavern and get herself well and truly killed. If that was what she wanted I had no right to prevent her. But if she had wanted to die, why hadn't she done the thing cleanly, registered her intention and gone to the medic, as anyone would? I didn't understand.

There was a good deal I didn't understand, and nineteen years pretending to be human hadn't taught me as much as I'd thought.

MOLL

From *Moll Flanders*

by Daniel Defoe

Moll Flanders becomes a 'wicked woman' by the standards of her day (the early eighteenth century). In the novel, she tells her own story and we see her admirable strength of character. By the time she comes to tell this story she has survived childhood poverty, been badly treated by an early lover, married twice, and lived amongst men who wanted to use her, but whom she resisted. From childhood she has had a dream of becoming a 'gentlewoman', by which she means simply a woman capable of earning her own living. Born in Newgate Prison, she had little understanding of what English gentility meant and how impossible it was for a woman born outside it, especially a 'fallen woman', to ever make a decent life for herself.

In this scene she gets it – how to do it. She comes to the conclusion that sex is commerce, and that poor women need to do business if they are to survive. There is a defiance in her tone at the end. This is a poor woman in a rich man's world who has finally figured out how to play the system.

It was now a merry time of the year, and Bartholomew Fair was begun. I had never made any walks that way, nor was the fair of much advantage to me; but I took a turn this year into the cloisters, and there I fell into one of the raffling shops. It was a thing of no great consequence to me, but there came a gentleman extremely well dressed and very rich, and as 'tis frequent to talk to everybody in those shops, he singled me out and was very particular with me. First he told me he would put in for me to raffle, and did so; and some small matter coming to his lot, he presented it to me – I think it was a feather muff; then he continued to keep talking to me with a more than common appearance of respect, but still very civil, and much like a gentleman.

He held me in talk so long, till at last he drew me out of the raffling place to the shop-door, and then to take a walk in the cloister, still talking of a thousand things cursorily without anything to the purpose. At last he told me that he was charmed with my company, and asked me if I durst trust myself in a coach with him; he told me he was a man of honour, and would not offer anything to me unbecoming him. I seemed to decline it a while, but suffered myself to be importuned a little, and then yielded.

I was at a loss in my thoughts to conclude at first what this gentleman designed; but I found afterward he had had some drink in his head, and that he was not very unwilling to have some more. He carried me to the Spring Garden, at Knightsbridge, where we walked in the gardens, and he treated me very handsomely; but I found he drank freely. He pressed me also to drink, but I declined it.

Hitherto he kept his word with me, and offered me nothing amiss. We came away in the coach again, and he brought me into the streets, and by this time it was near ten o'clock at night, when he stopped the coach at a house where, it seems, he was acquainted, and where they made no scruple to show us upstairs into a room with a bed in it. At first I seemed to be unwilling to go up, but after a few words I yielded to that too, being indeed willing to see the end of it, and in hopes to make something of it at last. As for the bed, etc., I was not much concerned about that part.

Here he began to be a little freer with me than he had promised; and I by little and little yielded to everything, so that, in a word, he did what he pleased with me; I need say no more. All this while he drank freely too, and about one in the morning we went into the coach again. The air and the shaking of the coach made the drink get more up in his head, and he grew uneasy, and was for acting over again what he had been doing before; but as I thought my game now secure, I resisted, and brought him to be a little still, which had not lasted five minutes but he fell fast asleep.

I took this opportunity to search him to a nicety. I took a gold watch, with a silk purse of gold, his fine full-bottom periwig and silver-fringed gloves, his sword and fine snuff-box, and gently opening the coach-door, stood ready to jump out while the coach was going on; but the coach stopping in the narrow street beyond Temple Bar to let another coach past, I got softly out, fastened the door again, and gave my gentleman and the coach the slip together.

This was an adventure indeed unlooked for, and perfectly undesigned by me; though I was not so past the merry part of life as to forget how to behave, when a fop so blinded by his appetite should not know an old woman from a young. I did not indeed look so old as I was by ten or twelve years; yet I was not a young wench of seventeen, and it was easy enough to be distinguished. There is nothing so absurd, so surfeiting, so ridiculous, as a man heated by wine in his head, and a wicked gust in his inclination together; he is in the possession of two devils at once, and can no more govern himself by his reason than a mill can grind without water; vice tramples upon all that was in him that had any good in it; nay, his very sense is blinded by his own rage, and he acts absurdities even in his view; such as drinking more, when he is drunk already; picking up a common woman, without any regard to what she is or who she is; whether sound or rotten, clean or unclean; whether ugly or handsome, old or young; and so blinded as not really to distinguish. Such a man is worse than lunatic; prompted by his vicious head, he no more knows what he is doing than this wretch of mine knew when I picked his pocket of his watch and his purse of gold.

These are the men of whom Solomon says, 'They go like an ox to the slaughter, till a dart strikes through their liver'; an admirable description, by the way, of the foul disease, which is a poisonous deadly contagion mingling with the blood, whose centre or fountain is in the liver; from whence, by the swift circulation of the whole mass, that dreadful nauseous plague strikes immediately through his liver, and his spirits are infected, his vitals stabbed through as with a dart.

It is true this poor unguarded wretch was in no danger from me, though I was greatly apprehensive at first what danger I might be in from him; but he was really to be pitied in one respect, that he seemed to be a good sort of man in himself: a gentleman that had no harm in his design; a man of sense, and of fine behaviour, a comely handsome person, a sober and solid countenance, a charming beautiful face, and everything that could be agreeable; only unhappily had some drink the night before; had not been in bed, as he told me when we were together; was hot, and his blood fired with wine, and in that condition his reason, as it were asleep, had given him up.

As for me, my business was his money, and what I could make of him;

and after that, if I could have found out any way to have done it, I would have sent him safe home to his house and to his family, for 'twas ten to one but he had an honest, virtuous wife and innocent children, that were anxious for his safety, and would have been glad to have gotten him home, and taken care of him, till he was restored to himself: and when with what shame and regret would he look back upon himself! how would he reproach himself with associating himself with a whore! picked up in the worst of all holes, the cloister, among the dirt and filth of the town! how would he be trembling for fear he had got the pox, for fear a dart had struck through his liver, and hate himself every time he looked back upon the madness and brutality of his debauch! how would he, if he had any principles of honour, abhor the thought of giving any ill distemper, if he had it, as for aught he knew he might, to his modest and virtuous wife, and thereby sowing the contagion in the life-blood of his posterity!

Would such gentlemen but consider the contemptible thoughts which the very women they are concerned with, in such cases as these, have of them, it would be a surfeit to them. They value not the pleasure, they are raised by no inclination to the man, the passive jade thinks of no pleasure but the money; and when he is, as it were, drunk in the ecstasies of his wicked pleasure, her hands are in his pockets for what she can find there.

PIP

From *Great Expectations*

by Charles Dickens

Pip was a poor boy brought into Miss Havisham's fine old house to be a companion for Estella, a lively young girl with whom he eventually falls in love. Miss Havisham is a bizarre old woman who was once jilted at the altar. She still wears her ragged old bridal gown and presides over the mouldy ruins of her abandoned wedding feast, which she has left untouched for many years.

At this point in the story, when he has grown up and returned to visit Miss Havisham and Estella, Pip innocently believes that Miss Havisham is the secret patroness of his recent success. It turns out that she is not, and, as we see in this scene, that she had adopted Estella in order to exact her revenge on men, and that Pip is her victim.

Pip is speaking here to the audience. It is the scene in which he first begins, in his naïve way, to understand what has been going on. He is telling us all this because he doesn't yet quite understand how dreadfully he has been deceived. He is moving from his young man's idea of love to an altogether older and more bitter one but, as he describes this, he only falteringly comes to an awareness of the real implications of what he is describing, perhaps not until after he delivers the last line.

You need to evoke, using the space around you, the three different locations: the country path where he loiters, the garden with Estella, and Miss Havisham's house.

The scene given here is extracted from Chapter 29, and has been edited.

In the morning I was up and out. It was too early yet to go to Miss Havisham's, so I loitered into the country on Miss Havisham's side of town – thinking about my patroness, and painting brilliant pictures of her plans for me.

She had adopted Estella, she had as good as adopted me, and it could not fail to be her intention to bring us together. I stopped to look at the house as I passed; and its seared red brick walls, blocked windows, and strong green ivy clasping even the stacks of chimneys with its twigs and tendons, as if with sinewy old arms, had made up a rich attractive mystery, of which I was the hero.

Estella was the inspiration of it, and the heart of it, of course. But, though she had taken such strong possession of me, though my fancy and my hope were so set upon her, though her influence on my boyish life and character had been all-powerful, I did not, even that romantic morning, invest her with any attributes save those she possessed.

When I loved Estella with the love of a man, I loved her simply because I found her irresistible. I knew to my sorrow, often and often, if not always, that I loved her against reason, against promise, against peace, against hope, against happiness, against all discouragement that could be. I loved her none the less because I knew it, and it had no more influence in restraining me than if I had devoutly believed her to be human perfection.

The air of completeness and superiority with which she walked at my side, and the air of youthfulness and submission with which I walked at hers, made a contrast that I strongly felt. It would have rankled in me more than it did, if I had not regarded myself as eliciting it by being so set apart for her and assigned to her.

The garden was too overgrown and rank for walking in with ease, and after we had made the round of it twice or thrice, we came out again into the brewery yard. I showed her to a nicety where I had seen her walking on the casks, that first old day, and she said, with a cold and careless look in that direction, 'Did I?' I reminded her where she had come out of the house and given me my meat and drink, and she said, 'I don't remember.' 'Not remember that you made me cry?' said I. 'No,' said she, and shook her head and looked about her. I verily believe that her not remembering and not minding in the least, made me cry again, inwardly,—and that is the sharpest crying of all.

'You must know,' said Estella, condescending to me as a brilliant and beautiful woman might, 'that I have no heart,—if that has anything to do with my memory.'

I got through some jargon to the effect that I took the liberty of doubting that. That I knew better. That there could be no such beauty without it.

'Oh! I have a heart to be stabbed in or shot in, I have no doubt,' said Estella, 'and of course if it ceased to beat I should cease to be. But you know what I mean. I have no softness there, no—sympathy—sentiment—nonsense.'

'I am serious,' said Estella, not so much with a frown (for her brow was smooth) as with a darkening of her face; 'if we are to be thrown much together, you had better believe it at once. No!' imperiously stopping me as I opened my lips. 'I have not bestowed my tenderness anywhere. I have never had any such thing.'

At last we went back into the house. The old wintry branches of chandeliers in the room where the mouldering table was spread had been lighted while we were out, and Miss Havisham was in her chair and waiting for me.

It was like pushing the chair itself back into the past, when we began the old slow circuit round about the ashes of the bridal feast. But, in the funereal room, with that figure of the grave fallen back in the chair fixing its eyes upon her, Estella looked more bright and beautiful than before, and I was under stronger enchantment.

The time so melted away, that our early dinner-hour drew close at hand, and Estella left us to prepare herself. We had stopped near the centre of the long table, and Miss Havisham, with one of her withered arms stretched out of the chair, rested that clenched hand upon the yellow cloth. As Estella looked back over her shoulder before going out at the door, Miss Havisham kissed that hand to her, with a ravenous intensity that was of its kind quite dreadful.

Then, Estella being gone and we two left alone, she turned to me, and said in a whisper,—

'Is she beautiful, graceful, well-grown? Do you admire her?'

'Everybody must who sees her, Miss Havisham.'

She drew an arm round my neck, and drew my head close down to hers as she sat in the chair. 'Love her, love her, love her! How does she use you?'

Before I could answer (if I could have answered so difficult a question at all) she repeated, 'Love her, love her, love her! If she favors you, love her. If she wounds you, love her. If she tears your heart to pieces,—and as it gets older and stronger it will tear deeper,—love her, love her, love her!'

Never had I seen such passionate eagerness as was joined to her utterance of these words. I could feel the muscles of the thin arm round my neck swell with the vehemence that possessed her.

'Hear me, Pip! I adopted her, to be loved. I bred her and educated her, to be loved. I developed her into what she is, that she might be loved. Love her!'

She said the word often enough, and there could be no doubt that she meant to say it; but if the often repeated word had been hate instead of love—despair—revenge—dire death—it could not have sounded from her lips more like a curse.

'I'll tell you,' said she, in the same hurried passionate whisper, 'what real love is. It is blind devotion, unquestioning self-humiliation, utter submission, trust and belief against yourself and against the whole world, giving up your whole heart and soul to the smiter—as I did!'

ALICE

From *Unpolished Gem*

by Alice Pung

In this memoir Alice recounts growing up as a Footscray (Melbourne) girl in a Cambodian–Chinese family. She is lively and funny in her telling of the clashes she experienced with her oppressive parents and grandparents. She is caught between two cultures. By this point of the book she has become an 'Asian High-Achiever', as she calls it, and has matriculated into Melbourne University to study to become a lawyer. She is eighteen years old.

At university she meets an Anglo named Michael, who obviously likes her. In her parents' culture you cannot date, romantic relationships are arranged by the parents and girls are kept at home until the arrangements are made; but in her Australian culture you choose yourself who to date and fall in love with. This is the conflict that underlies this piece. But she thinks he's cute, and this should be clear from the way she plays the opening dialogue. She enters enthusiastically into her theatrical re-enactments of the scenes on the street and in the restaurant, but then stands back outside them to comment and worry.

In this edited extract the passages in italics are her inner voices. The passages in plain text are her narration and her performance of the actual encounters with Michael.

'Wow,' he breathed as we emerged from the station onto the street. The sky was slowly turning the colour of a three-day-old bruise, and the streets were wet.

I stopped walking and turned to face him.

'Come on, please get back on the train and go home.'

'Go home?' he cried in mock mortification, complete with hands-to-the face demonstration. 'Oh! I'm doing the chivalrous thing by escorting you back through these brutal streets and you tell me to nick off?'

'Well, I've managed for eighteen years by myself, I think I should be fine for one more day.'

'Go home?' he cried. 'You have no idea! I can't possibly go home.'

'Yes, you can. You have a Daily Metcard which expires at 2 a.m.'

'Ohhh, please don't make me go back! I can't!'

'Why not?'

'Because I've journeyed perilously by train to get here, wedged between disease-carrying passengers and surviving only by clinging to a hand-rail with three fingers! Please don't send me back! Oh, such suffering I have endured to get here!'

As moved as I was by his miserable odyssey, I had to tell him that *we* weren't parading our suffering by moaning about landmines and leaking boats. [...]

'What time does your dad's shop close tonight?' he asked.

'Nine o'clock. It's Friday – late night trading.'

'Errr ... it's only six-thirty at the moment.' He had stopped in front of a shopfront with neon lettering on the outside declaring Hai Duong Vietnamese noodles. Mr Hai Duong himself was probably inside declaring, 'Wah, isn't that the Newtone Electronics daughter and what is she doing loitering with scruffy white demons?'

He looked at me. 'Umm ... want to grab some dinner then?'

I hesitated, and tried to think clearly.

He really likes you, I told myself.

No way, he likes the idea of you, the less feeble part of my mind insisted, *he's probably a sinophile. Don't forget that he's doing an Asian Studies major. You're like his third-world trip or something. He's too broke to go overseas so you're his substitute exotic experience. You go to dinner with him now and he'll think you're going to be his Cherry Chrysanthemum forever, or at least until he gets bored of you and the next little Oriental Oleander comes along. Then you're going to be sorry.*

Bugger, what'll I do?

How the hell am I meant to know, I've never been on a 'date' before! But you're not going to last long, if you keep using words like bugger, because authentic Chinese chicks don't speak like that, you sound like a bloody ocker.

Well, what am I supposed to do?

Firstly, stop having this dialogue inside your head because he'll realise that you're not only slow but insane too. Secondly, tell him no, tell him he's a show-off and a sinophile only interested in your ethnicity, tell him you don't do conventional Karate-Kid-Part-II *romances, tell him you have to head back before it gets dark, tell him you have to help your father sell Walkmans, tell him you have to go to the May Madness Sale at Forges to buy plastic tofu boxes for your mother, tell him that you have to go to the local pool before closing time to check out those fabulous homeboys getting changed into their flannelette shirts and trousers before they retreat back to their com-pu-tahs, tell him you have to find a way to dispose of those Indochinese interlopers who stare at you and report back to your relatives when you eventually tell him …*

'Umm, yeah, okay.'

Bugger.

After all, what's the big deal? I reasoned to myself, *have some humility. A young man casually mentions that you might have dinner together and you think he's asking for your hand, you think you're going to end up his little Indochinese wife and in a decade's time you won't be fascinating anymore because he's just drawn to the idiosyncrasies of your culture, and he has no idea that your culture extends to looking after your folks in their decrepit dotage and constantly looking out for ASIO which has caused you to develop a nasty compulsive head-swivelling habit. And of course he has no idea that ASIO really stands for Asian (Southeast) Investigation Organisation, but if you tell him, perhaps one day when you've both graduated, he can help you sue the organisation for causing you chronic pain and suffering…*

I was still not convinced.

Oh, come on, Voice of Reason cajoled, *you're turning into one of those anxious killjoy Asian women who worry so much that they end up with dried-fig faces at the age of thirty; come on, you're only eighteen, just sit down, just relax, just have dinner, and don't take things so seriously.*

So we entered the mirror-walled, plastic Ikea-chaired surroundings of Hai Duong, and when we sat down, he asked me: 'What will your father say when I ask you to be my girlfriend?' […]

I wanted to know whether it was only because I was 'exotic', and if so, what that word meant to him. If he told me he liked my almond eyes and my caramel skin, I would tell him to buy a bag of confectionery instead, because I was sick of it all – how we always had to have hair like a black waterfall, alabaster or porcelain skin, and some body part or other resembling a peach. I wanted to ask him whether one of his reasons for going out with me was to test out the rumour about Asian girls' gynaecological advantages. And finally, I wanted to know why, out of all the girls in his college who liked him, he had picked me. [...]

'No.'

'What do you mean, no?'

'I can't.' *Great. Now you sound like a fifteen-year-old loser whose parents won't let her go out. What are you going to say now? 'It's not you, it's* me?' *Oh, but it was so true!*

We both sat there looking pretty tormented. When our food arrived, we let the noodles soak. He half-heartedly plonked in a spoon.

'You know, I don't know how to do this.'

'Don't worry, they automatically lower the MSG content for Caucasians and you can use a fork.'

'No! I mean, I've never ... you know, asked anyone ... like ... well, you know ...'

'Oh.'

'Perhaps I've gone about it the wrong way. I'm an idiot. Sorry, I've mucked it up. Crap.'

'No, you haven't. I think *I've* mucked it up.' I paused, and realised that I didn't say these words merely to make him feel better either. I wanted to cry. This was terrible and confusing and I had mucked it up by thinking too much, and now I had hurt this poor amateur Asian-asker-outer by frightening myself with fears before anything had even happened.

'Well ...' I said, and paused. Where could I begin?

'Err ...' I began again. How could I begin? Oh, what to say? Oh, what to do?

Luckily he came up with a simple solution.

'Ummm ... can we un-muck it then?'

Anything to get rid of this sudden sinking feeling I had in my gut, this feeling of cowardice. This feeling of missing out on something I wasn't even sure I wanted. But worst of all, this feeling of missing out on something I might have chosen for myself.

'Okay.'

ELENA

From *My Brilliant Friend*

by Elena Ferrante

This is an edited extract taken from the end of the first of a series of four novels. They are all centred around Elena and Lila, who have been troubled best friends since they were five. Here they are sixteen. The series follows their lives until they are in their sixties.

Here Elena is with Lila on the morning of Lila's wedding, and then at the ceremony itself. The transition in time happens after the line, 'What's going to happen to me, Lenu?'

They have both grown up in a poor outer suburb of Naples. It is the 1960s. It seems to them impossible to break out of their class, but they are both trying: Lila through marriage and Elena through education.

Elena is narrating her memories from many decades on, but you need not play it that way. Her journey is the hope that they want, somehow, together, to enter a new and better world, and then the sudden realisation that this will be very hard.

This scene leaves out a lot of the novelistic detail but you should be able to play the significance of the ending. The Solara brothers are Camorra Mafia and the fact that Marcello Solara is wearing the shoes Lila made with her brother is the first sign that her husband has joined them. It is a huge betrayal by him, especially on their wedding night. Certainly it should be clear to the audience that the sudden intrusion of the Solara brothers is deeply shocking to Lila.

March 12th arrived, a mild day that was almost like spring. Lila wanted me to come early to her old house, so that I could help her wash, do her hair, dress. She sent her mother away, we were alone. She sat on the edge of the bed in underpants and bra. Next to her was the wedding dress, which looked like the body of a dead woman; in front of us, on the hexagonal-tiled floor, was the copper tub full of boiling water. She asked me abruptly: 'Do you think I'm making a mistake?'

'How?'

'By getting married.' […]

She was silent for a while, staring at the water that sparkled in the tub, then she said, 'Whatever happens, you'll go on studying.'

'Two more years: then I'll get my diploma and I'm done.'

'No, don't ever stop: I'll give you the money, you should keep studying.'

I gave a nervous laugh, then said, 'Thanks, but at a certain point school is over.'

'Not for you: you're my brilliant friend, you have to be the best of all, boys and girls.'

She got up, took off her underpants and bra, said, 'Come on, help me, otherwise I'll be late.'

I had never seen her naked, I was embarrassed. Today I can say that it was the embarrassment of gazing with pleasure at her body, of being the not impartial witness of her sixteen-year-old's beauty a few hours before Stefano touched her, penetrated her, disfigured her, perhaps, by making her pregnant. At the time it was just a tumultuous sensation of necessary awkwardness, a state in which you cannot avert the gaze or take away the hand without recognizing your own turmoil, without, by that retreat, declaring it, hence without coming into conflict with the undisturbed innocence of the one who is the cause of the turmoil, without expressing by that rejection the violent emotion that overwhelms you, so that it forces you to stay, to rest your gaze on the childish shoulders, on the breasts and stiffly cold nipples, on the narrow hips and the tense buttocks, on the black sex, on the long legs, on the tender knees, on the curved ankles, on the elegant feet; and to act as if it's nothing, when instead everything is there, present, in the poor dim room, amid the worn furniture, on the uneven, water-stained floor, and your heart is agitated, your veins inflamed.

I washed her with slow, careful gestures, first letting her squat in the tub, then asking her to stand up: I still have in my ears the sound of the dripping water, and the impression that the copper of the tub had a consistency not different from Lila's flesh, which was smooth, solid, calm. I had a confusion of feelings and thoughts: embrace her, weep with her, kiss her, pull her hair, laugh, pretend to sexual experience and instruct her in a learned voice, distancing her with words just at the moment of greatest closeness. But in the end there was only the hostile thought that I was washing her, from her hair to the soles of her feet, early in the morning, just so that Stefano could sully her in the course of the night. I imagined her naked as she was at that moment, entwined with her husband, in the bed in the new house, while the train clattered under their window and his violent flesh entered her with a sharp blow, like the cork pushed by the palm into the neck of a wine bottle. And it suddenly seemed to me, that the only remedy against the pain I was feeling, that I would feel, was to find a corner secluded enough so that Antonio could do to me, at the same time, the exact same thing.

I helped her dry off, dress, put on the wedding dress that I – I, I thought with a mixture of pride and suffering – had chosen for her. The fabric became living, over its whiteness ran Lila's heat, the red of her mouth, her hard black eyes. Finally she put on the shoes that she herself had designed. Pressed by [her brother] Rino, who if she hadn't worn them would have felt a kind of betrayal, she had chosen a pair with low heels, to avoid seeming too much taller than Stefano. She looked at herself in the mirror, lifting the dress slightly.

'They're ugly,' she said.

'It's not true.'

She laughed nervously.

'But yes, look: the mind's dreams have ended up under the feet.'

She turned with a sudden expression of fear.

'What's going to happen to me, Lenu?' [...]

We were sixteen. I was sitting with Nino Sarratore, Afonso, Marisa, and I made an effort to smile. Lila was at the other end of the room – she was the bride, the queen of the celebration – and Stefano was whispering in her ear and she was smiling.

The long, exhausting wedding lunch was ending. The band was playing, the singer was singing. Antonio, with his back to me, was suppressing in his chest the pain I had caused him, and looking at the sea. Enzo was perhaps murmuring to Carmela that he loved her. Rino certainly had already done so with Pinuccia, who, as she talked, was staring into his eyes. Pasquale in all likelihood was wandering around frightened, but Ada would manage so that, before the party was over, she would tear out of his mouth the necessary words. For a while toasts with obscene allusions had been tumbling out. The floor was splattered with sauces from a plate dropped by a child, wine spilled by Stefano's grandfather. I swallowed my tears.

[Our teacher once asked me,] 'Do you know what the plebs are?' 'Yes, Maestra.' At that moment I knew what the plebs were. The plebs were us. The plebs were that fight for food and wine, that quarrel over who should be served first and better, that dirty floor on which the waiters clattered back and forth, those increasingly vulgar toasts. The plebs were my mother, who had drunk wine and now was leaning against my father's shoulder, while he, serious, laughed, his mouth gaping, at the sexual allusions. They were all laughing, even Lila, with the expression of one who has a role and will play it to the utmost. [...]

Later I had the impression that a gust of wind had shut the door of the restaurant. In reality there was no wind or even a banging of doors. There happened only what could have been predicted to happen. Just in time for the cake, for the favors, the very handsome, very well-dressed Solara brothers appeared. They moved through the room greeting this one and that in their lordly way. Rino with a friendly smile invited Marcello to sit down. Marcello sat down, loosened his tie, crossed his legs.

The unpredictable revealed itself only at that point. I saw Lila lose her color, become as pale as when she was a child, whiter than her wedding dress, and her eyes had that sudden contraction that turned them into cracks. She had in front of her a bottle of wine and I was afraid that her gaze would go through it with a violence that would shatter it, with the wine spraying everywhere. But she wasn't looking at the bottle. She was looking farther away, she was looking at the shoes of Marcello Solara.

They were Cerullo shoes for men. Not the model for sale, not the ones with the gilded pin. Marcello had on his feet the shoes, bought earlier by Stefano, her husband. It was the pair she had made with [her brother], making and unmaking them for months, ruining her hands.

MOLLY

From *Ulysses*

by James Joyce

This is the most challenging piece in this book to prepare for performance, but it has been performed many times and is enormously rewarding. A range of performances of this piece can be found on YouTube. It is the final section of one of the greatest soliloquies ever written. It is printed here as it is in the novel, with no punctuation at all except for the final full stop (which you can play with in performance). You have to find the sense of it yourself, as you prepare it.

Molly is Irish and this is a stream of consciousness, in which Joyce has tried to create everything that goes on in her head as she lies in bed with her husband, Leopold Bloom, asleep beside her after his long day roaming the streets of Dublin. The novel has many parallels with the Homeric ancient Greek story of Ulysses (Odysseus) and his long-suffering wife Penelope, who waited ten years for the Trojan Wars to end and then another ten years for him to finally get home.

Here Molly remembers her lover, thinks about her husband and her dead son, and has other dreams and fantasies. What we have given you here is about three times longer than you could do in a standard audition piece, but it is worth reading right through. We have inserted an asterisk at places where it might be broken into manageable lengths but the text of the original is continuous. You can cut or edit it any way you like.

It is an extraordinarily rich piece of writing. If you read bits of it aloud to yourself, in an Irish accent, you'll soon see the glory of it.

no thats no way for him has he no manners nor no refinement nor no nothing in his nature slapping us behind like that on my bottom because I didnt call him Hugh the ignoramus that doesnt know poetry from a cabbage thats what you get for not keeping them in their proper place pulling off his shoes and trousers there on the chair before me so barefaced without even asking permission and standing out that vulgar way in the half of a shirt they wear to be admired like a priest or a butcher or those old hypocrites in the time of Julius Caesar of course hes right enough in his way to pass the time as a joke sure you might as well be in bed with what with a lion God Im sure hed have something better to say for himself an old Lion would O well I suppose its because they were so plump and tempting in my short petticoat he couldnt resist they excite myself sometimes its well for men all the amount of pleasure they get off a womans body were so round and white for them always I wished I was one myself for a change just to try with that thing they have swelling upon you so hard and at the same time so soft when you touch it my uncle John has a thing long I heard those cornerboys saying passing the corner of Marrowbone lane my aunt Mary has a thing hairy because it was dark and they knew a girl was passing it didnt make me blush why should it either its only nature and he puts his thing long into my aunt Marys hairy etcetera and turns out to be you put the handle in a sweepingbrush men again all over they can pick and choose what they please a married woman or a fast widow or a girl for their different tastes like those houses round behind Irish street no but were to be always chained up theyre not going to be chaining me up no damn fear once I start I tell you for stupid husbands jealousy why cant we all remain friends over it instead of quarrelling her husband found it out what they did together well naturally and if he did can he undo it hes coronado anyway whatever he does and then he going to the other mad extreme about the wife in Fair Tyrants of course the man never even casts a 2nd thought on the husband or wife either its the woman he wants and he gets her what else were we given all those desires for Id like to know I cant help it if Im young still can I its a wonder Im not an old shrivelled hag before my time living with him so cold never embracing me except sometimes when hes asleep the wrong end of me not knowing I suppose who he has any man thatd kiss a womans bottom Id throw my hat at him after that hed kiss anything unnatural where we havent 1 atom of any kind of expression in us all of us the same 2 lumps of lard before ever Id do that to a man pfooh the dirty brutes the mere thought is enough I kiss the feet of you senorita theres some sense in that didnt he kiss our halldoor yes he did what a madman nobody understands his cracked ideas but me still of course a woman wants to be embraced 20 times a day almost to make her look young no matter by who so long as to be in love or loved by somebody if the fellow you want isnt there sometimes by the Lord God I was thinking would I go around by the quays there some dark evening where nobodyd know me and pick up a sailor off the sea thatd be hot on for it and not care a pin whose I was only do it off up in a gate somewhere or one of those wildlooking gipsies in Rathfarnham had their camp pitched near the Bloomfield laundry to try and steal our things if they could I only sent mine there a few times for the name model laundry sending me back over and over some old ones old stockings that blackguardlooking fellow with the fine eyes peeling a switch attack me in the dark and ride me up against the wall without a word or a murderer anybody what they do themselves the fine gentlemen in their silk hats that K C lives up somewhere this way coming out of Hardwicke lane the night he gave us the fish supper on account of winning over the boxing match of course it was for me he gave it I knew him by his gaiters and the walk and when I turned round a minute after just to see there was a woman after coming out of it too some filthy prostitute then he goes home to his wife after that only I suppose the half of those sailors are rotten again with disease O move over your big carcass out of that for the love of Mike listen to him the winds that waft my sighs to thee so well he may sleep and sigh the great Suggester Don Poldo de la Flora if he knew how he came out on the cards this morning hed have something to sigh for a dark man in some perplexity between 2 7s too in prison for Lord knows what he does that I dont know and Im to be slooching around down in the kitchen to get his lordship his breakfast while hes rolled up like a mummy will I indeed did you ever see me running Id just like to see myself at it show them attention and they treat you like dirt I dont care what anybody says itd be much better for the world to be governed by the women in it you wouldnt see women going and killing one another and slaughtering

*

when do you ever see women rolling around drunk like they do or gambling every penny they have and losing it on horses yes because a woman whatever she does she knows where to stop sure they wouldnt be in the world at all only for us they dont know what it is to be a woman and a mother how could they where would they all of them be if they hadnt all a mother to look after them what I never had thats why I suppose hes running wild now out at night away from his books and studies and not living at home on account of the usual rowy house I suppose well its a poor case that those that have a fine son like that theyre not satisfied and I none was he not able to make one it wasnt my fault we came together when I was watching the two dogs up in her behind in the middle of the naked street that disheartened me altogether I suppose I oughtnt to have buried him in that little woolly jacket I knitted crying as I was but give it to some poor child but I knew well Id never have another our 1st death too it was we were never the same since O Im not going to think myself into the glooms about that any more I wonder why he wouldnt stay the night I felt all the time it was somebody strange he brought in instead of roving around the city meeting God knows who nightwalkers and pickpockets his poor mother wouldnt like that if she was alive ruining himself for life perhaps still its a lovely hour so silent I used to love coming home after dances the air of the night they have friends they can talk to weve none either he wants what he wont get or its some woman ready to stick her knife in you I hate that in women no wonder they treat us the way they do we are a dreadful lot of bitches I suppose its all the troubles we have makes us so snappy Im not like that he could easy have slept in there on the sofa in the other room I suppose he was as shy as a boy he being so young hardly 20 of me in the next room hed have heard me on the chamber arrah what harm Dedalus I wonder its like those names in Gibraltar Delapaz Delagracia they had the devils queer names there father Vilaplana of Santa Maria that gave me the rosary Rosales y OReilly in the Calle las Siete Revueltas and Pisimbo and Mrs Opisso in Governor street O what a name Id go and drown myself in the first river if I had a name like her O my and all the bits of streets Paradise ramp and Bedlam ramp and Rodgers ramp and Crutchetts ramp and the devils gap steps well small blame to me if I am a harumscarum I know I am a bit I declare to God I dont feel a day older than then I wonder could I get my tongue round any of the Spanish como esta usted muy bien gracias y usted see I havent forgotten it all I thought I had only for the grammar a noun is the name of any person placc or thing pity I never tried to read that novel cantankerous Mrs Rubio lent me by Valera with the questions in it all upside down the two ways I always knew wed go away in the end I can tell him the Spanish and he tell me the Italian then hell see Im not so ignorant what a pity he didnt stay Im sure the poor fellow was dead tired and wanted a good sleep badly I could have brought him in his breakfast in bed with a bit of toast so long as I didnt do it on the knife for bad luck or if the woman was going her rounds with the watercress and something nice and tasty there are a few olives in the kitchen he might like I never could bear the look of them in Abrines I could do the criada the room looks all right since I changed it the other way you see something was telling me all the time Id have to introduce myself not knowing me from Adam very funny wouldnt it Im his wife or pretend we were in Spain with him half awake without a Gods notion where he is dos huevos estrellados senor Lord the cracked things come into my head sometimes itd be great fun supposing he stayed with us why not theres the room upstairs empty and Millys bed in the back room he could do his writing and studies at the table in there for all the scribbling he does at it and if he wants to read in bed in the morning like me as hes making the breakfast for 1 he can make it for 2 Im sure Im not going to take in lodgers off the street for him if he takes a gesabo of a house like this Id love to have a long talk with an intelligent welleducated person Id have to get a nice pair of red slippers like those Turks with the fez used to sell or yellow and a nice semitransparent morning gown that I badly want or a peachblossom dressing jacket like the one long ago in Walpoles only 8/6 or 18/6 Ill just give him one more chance Ill get up early in the morning Im sick of Cohens old bed in any case I might go over to the markets to see all the vegetables and cabbages and tomatoes and carrots and all kinds of splendid fruits all coming in lovely and fresh who knows whod be the 1st man Id meet theyre out looking for it in the morning Mamy Dillon used to say they are and the night too that was her massgoing Id love a big juicy pear now to melt in your mouth like when I used to be in the longing way then Ill throw him up his eggs and tea in the moustachecup she gave him to make his mouth bigger I suppose hed like my nice cream too I know what Ill do Ill go about rather gay not too much singing a bit now and then mi fa pieta Masetto then Ill start dressing myself to go out presto non son piu forte Ill put on my best shift and drawers let him have a good eyeful out of that to make his micky stand for him Ill let him know if thats what he wanted that his wife is fucked yes and damn well fucked too up to my neck nearly not by him 5 or 6 times handrunning theres the mark of his spunk on the clean sheet I wouldnt bother to even iron it out that ought to satisfy him if you dont believe me feel my belly

*

unless I made him stand there and put him into me Ive a mind to tell him every scrap and make him do it out in front of me serve him right its all his own fault if I am an adulteress as the thing in the gallery said O much about it if thats all the harm ever we did in this vale of tears God knows its not much doesnt everybody only they hide it I suppose thats what a woman is supposed to be there for or He wouldnt have made us the way He did so attractive to men then if he wants to kiss my bottom Ill drag open my drawers and bulge it right out in his face as large as life he can stick his tongue 7 miles up my hole as hes there my brown part then Ill tell him I want 1 or perhaps 30/– Ill tell him I want to buy underclothes then if he gives me that well he wont be too bad I dont want to soak it all out of him like other women do I could often have written out a fine cheque for myself and write his name on it for a couple of pounds a few times he forgot to lock it up besides he wont spend it Ill let him do it off on me behind provided he doesnt smear all my good drawers O I suppose that cant be helped Ill do the indifferent 1 or 2 questions Ill know by the answers when hes like that he cant keep a thing back I know every turn in him Ill tighten my bottom well and let out a few smutty words smellrump or lick my shit or the first mad thing comes into my head then Ill suggest about yes O wait now sonny my turn is coming Ill be quite gay and friendly over it O but I was forgetting this bloody pest of a thing pfooh you wouldnt know which to laugh or cry were such a mixture of plum and apple no Ill have to wear the old things so much the better itll be more pointed hell never know whether he did it or not there thats good enough for you any old thing at all then Ill wipe him off me just like a business his omission then Ill go out Ill have him eying up at the ceiling where is she gone now make him want me thats the only way a quarter after what an unearthly hour I suppose theyre just getting up in China now combing out their pigtails for the day well soon have the nuns ringing the angelus theyve nobody coming in to spoil their sleep except an odd priest or two for his night office or the alarmclock next door at cockshout clattering the brains out of itself let me see if I can doze off 1 2 3 4 5 what kind of flowers are those they invented like the stars the wallpaper in Lombard street was much nicer the apron he gave me was like that something only I only wore it twice better lower this lamp and try again so as I can get up early Ill go to Lambes there beside Findlaters and get them to send us some flowers to put about the place in case he brings him home tomorrow today I mean no no Fridays an unlucky day first I want to do the place up someway the dust grows in it I think while Im asleep then we can have music and cigarettes I can accompany him first I must clean the keys of the piano with milk whatll I wear shall I wear a white rose or those fairy cakes in Liptons I love the smell of a rich big shop at 7 1/2d a lb or the other ones with the cherries in them and the pinky sugar 11d a couple of lbs of those a nice plant for the middle of the table Id get that cheaper in wait wheres this I saw them not long ago I love flowers Id love to have the whole place swimming in roses God of heaven theres nothing like nature the wild mountains then the sea and the waves rushing then the beautiful country with fields of oats and wheat and all kinds of things and all the fine cattle going about that would do your heart good to see rivers and lakes and flowers all sorts of shapes and smells and colours springing up even out of the ditches primroses and violets nature it is as for them saying theres no God I wouldnt give a snap of my two fingers for all their learning why dont they go and create something I often asked him atheists or whatever they call themselves go and wash the cobbles off themselves first then they go howling for the priest and they dying and why why because theyre afraid of hell on account of their bad conscience ah yes I know them well who was the first person in the universe before there was anybody that made it all who ah that they dont know neither do I so there you are they might as well try to stop the sun from rising tomorrow the sun shines for you he said the day we were lying among the rhododendrons on Howth head in the grey tweed suit and his straw hat the day I got him to propose to me yes first I gave him the bit of seedcake out of my mouth and it was leapyear like now yes 16 years ago my God after that long kiss I near lost my breath yes he said I was a flower of the mountain yes so we are flowers all a womans body yes that was one true thing he said in his life and the sun shines for you today yes that was why I liked him because I saw he understood or felt what a woman is and I knew I could always get round him and I gave him all the pleasure I could leading him on till he asked me to say yes and I wouldnt answer first only looked out over the sea and the sky I was thinking of so many things he didnt know of Mulvey and Mr Stanhope and Hester and father and old captain Groves and the sailors playing all birds fly and I say stoop and washing up dishes they called it on the pier and the sentry in front of the governors house with the thing round his white helmet poor devil half roasted and the Spanish girls laughing in their shawls and their tall combs and the auctions in the morning the Greeks and the jews and the Arabs and the devil knows who else from all the ends of Europe and Duke street and the fowl market all clucking outside Larby Sharons and the poor donkeys slipping half asleep and the vague fellows in the cloaks asleep in the shade on the steps and the big wheels of the carts of the bulls and the old castle thousands of years old yes and those handsome Moors all in white and turbans like kings asking you to sit down in their little bit of a shop and Ronda with the old windows of the posadas glancing eyes a lattice hid for her lover to kiss the iron and the wineshops half open at night and the castanets and the night we missed the boat at Algeciras the watchman going about serene with his lamp and O that awful deepdown torrent O and the sea the sea crimson sometimes like fire and the glorious sunsets and the figtrees in the Alameda gardens yes and all the queer little streets and the pink and blue and yellow houses and the rosegardens and the jessamine and geraniums and cactuses and Gibraltar as a girl where I was a Flower of the mountain yes when I put the rose in my hair like the Andalusian girls used or shall I wear a red yes and how he kissed me under the Moorish wall and I thought well as well him as another and then I asked him with my eyes to ask again yes and then he asked me would I yes to say yes my mountain flower and first I put my arms around him yes and drew him down to me so he could feel my breasts all perfume yes and his heart was going like mad and yes I said yes I will Yes.

JANE

From *Jane Eyre*

by Charlotte Bronte

This is a slightly edited and re-paragraphed version of Jane's decision to refuse a good and worthy man whom she doesn't love. In the novel the implication is that she will wait for the difficult man that she does love: Mr Rochester. St. John (pronounced 'Sin-jen') has just asked her to marry him and accompany him to India to do 'God's work'. Jane's action here, in performance, is that she really cares for St. John, and so it pains her to reject him. She does so because she cannot love him, and she thinks that that is what a true marriage entails. The fact that she is even prepared, for a moment, to contemplate spending the rest of her life in India with him is a sign of her integrity.

There is an element of disdain in the way she plays St. John's lines, perhaps. He is placed on stage somewhere, in her imagination. She comes to understand the pompous patriarchal assumptions that underlie his arguments, although she would not put it like that, of course.

I *can* do what he wants me to do: I am forced to see and acknowledge that, that is, if life be spared me. But I feel mine is not the existence to be long protracted under an Indian sun. What then? He does not care for that: when my time came to die, he would resign me, in all serenity and sanctity, to the God who gave me. The case is very plain before me. In leaving England, I should leave a loved but empty land – Mr Rochester is not there; and if we were, what is, what can that ever be to me? My business is to live without him now: nothing so absurd, so weak as to drag on from day to day, as if I were waiting some impossible change in circumstances, which might reunite me to him. Of course (as St. John once said) I must seek another interest in life to replace the one lost: is not the occupation he now offers me truly the most glorious man can adopt or God assign? Is it not, by its noble cares and sublime results, the one best calculated to fill the void left by uptorn affections and demolished hopes. I believe I must say Yes – and yet I shudder.

Alas! If I join St. John, I abandon half myself: if I go to India, I go to premature death. And how will the interval between leaving England for India, and India for the grave, be filled? Oh, I know well! That, too, is very clear to my vision. By straining to satisfy St. John till my sinews ache, I *shall* satisfy him – to the finest central point and farthest outward circle of his expectations. If I *do* go with him – if I *do* make the sacrifice he urges, I will make it absolutely: I will throw all on the altar – heart, vitals, the entire victim. He will never love me; but he shall approve me; I will show him energies he has not yet seen, resources he has never suspected. Yes, I can work as hard as he can, and with as little grudging.

Consent, then, to his demand is possible: but for one item – one dreadful item. It is – that he asks me to be his wife, and has no more of a husband's heart for me than that frowning giant of a rock, down which the stream is foaming in yonder gorge. He prizes me as a soldier would a good weapon, and that is all. Unmarried to him, this would never grieve me; but can I let him complete his calculations – coolly put into practice his plans – go through the wedding ceremony? Can I receive from him the bridal ring, endure all the forms of love (which I doubt not he would scrupulously observe) and know that the spirit was quite absent? Can I bear the consciousness that every endearment he bestows is a sacrifice made on principle? No: such a martyrdom would be monstrous. I will never undergo it. As his sister, I might accompany him – not as his wife: I will tell him so.

I looked towards the knoll: there he lay, still as a prostrate column; his face turned to me; his eye beaming watchful and keen. He started to his feet and approached me.

'I am ready to go to India, if I may go free.'

'Your answer requires a commentary,' he said; 'it is not clear.'

'You have hitherto been my adopted brother – I, your adopted sister: let us continue as such: you and I had better not marry.'

He shook his head. 'Adopted fraternity will not do in this case. If you were my real sister it would be different; I should take you, and seek no wife. But as it is, either our union must be consecrated and sealed by marriage, or it cannot exist: practical obstacles oppose themselves to any other plan. Do you not see it, Jane? Consider a moment – your strong sense will guide you.'

I did consider; and still my sense, such as it was, directed me only to the fact that we did not love each other as man and wife should: and therefore it inferred we ought not to marry. I said so. 'St. John,' I returned, 'I regard you as a brother – you, me as a sister: so let us continue.'

'We cannot – we cannot,' he answered, with short, sharp determination: 'it would not do. You have said you will go with me to India: remember – you have said that.'

'Conditionally.'

'Well – well. To the main point – the departure with me from England, the co-operation with me in my future labours – you do not object. You have already as good as put your hand to the plough: you are too consistent to withdraw it. You have but one end to keep in view – how the work you have undertaken can best be done. Simplify your complicated interests, feelings, thoughts, wishes, aims; merge all considerations in one purpose: that of fulfilling with effect – with power – the mission of your great Master. To do so, you must have a coadjutor: not a brother – that is a loose tie – but a husband. I, too, do not want a sister: a sister might any day be taken from me. I want a wife: the sole helpmeet I can influence efficiently in life, and retain absolutely till death.'

I shuddered as he spoke: I felt his influence in my marrow – his hold on my limbs.

'Seek one elsewhere than in me, St. John: seek one fitted to you.'

'One fitted to my purpose, you mean – fitted to my vocation. Again I tell you it is not the insignificant private individual – the mere man, with the man's selfish senses – I wish to mate: it is the missionary.'

'And I will give the missionary my energies – it is all he wants – but not myself: that would be only adding the husk and shell to the kernel. For them he has no use: I retain them.'

'You cannot – you ought not. Do you think God will be satisfied with half an oblation? Will He accept a mutilated sacrifice? It is the cause of God

I advocate: it is under His standard I enlist you. I cannot accept on His behalf a divided allegiance: it must be entire.'

'Oh! I will give my heart to God,' I said. '*You* do not want it.'

MYRNA'S HUSBAND

From 'Mr Coffee and Mr Fixit', in *What We Talk About When We Talk About Love* by Raymond Carver

This is a complete piece with no context other than what is implied in the text. It is full of sad comedy and has many layers. The speaker is talking to the audience. He tells us of a surprise encounter with his mother; and then of his reaction to his wife's affair. Underlying his account of the relationship between her and 'Mr Fixit' is the fact, which we only learn at the end, that in spite of all their troubles Myrna has come back to him now.

He is a simple man, and sometimes seems not to understand the significance of what he is saying. He just wants to understand people and to be loved, although he is not very good at either. There is a great deal that is hinted at in his references to the drinking and the friendships, and a lot of emotional subtext in the small details that he recounts.

I've seen some things. I was going over to my mother's to stay a few nights. But just as I got to the top of the stairs, I looked and she was on the sofa kissing a man. It was summer. The door was open. The TV was going. That's one of the things I've seen.

My mother is sixty-five. She belongs to a singles club. Even so, it was hard. I stood with my hand on the railing and watched as the man kissed her. She was kissing him back, and the TV was going.

Things are better now. But back in those days, when my mother was putting out, I was out of work. My kids were crazy, and my wife was crazy. She was putting out too. The guy that was getting it was an unemployed aerospace engineer she'd met at AA. He was also crazy.

His name was Ross and he had six kids. He walked with a limp from a gunshot wound his first wife gave him.

I didn't know what we were thinking of in those days.

This guy's second wife had come and gone, but it was his first wife who had shot him for not meeting his payments. I wish him well now. Ross. What a name! But it was different then. In those days I mentioned weapons. I'd say to my wife, 'I think I'll get a Smith and Wesson.' But I never did it.

Ross was a little guy. But not too little. He had a moustache and always wore a button-up sweater.

His one wife jailed him once. The second one did. I found out from my daughter that my wife went bail. My daughter Melody didn't like it any better than I did. About the bail. It wasn't that Melody was looking out for me. She wasn't looking out for either one of us, her mother or me neither. It was just that there was a serious cash thing and if some of it went to Ross, there'd be that much less for Melody. So Ross was on Melody's list. Also, she didn't like his kids, and his having so many of them. But in general Melody said Ross was all right.

He'd even told her fortune once.

This Ross guy spent his time repairing things, now that he had no regular job. But I'd seen his house from the outside. It was a mess. Junk all around. Two busted Plymouths in the yard.

In the first stages of the thing they had going, my wife claimed the guy collected antique cars. Those were her words, 'antique cars'. But they were just clunkers.

I had his number, Mr Fixit.

But we had things in common, Ross and me, which was more than just the same woman. For example, he couldn't fix the TV when it went crazy and we lost the picture. I couldn't fix it either. We had volume, but no picture. If we wanted the news, we had to sit around the screen and listen.

Ross and Myrna met when Myrna was trying to stay sober. She was going to meetings, I'd say, three or four times a week. I had been in and out myself. But when Myrna met Ross, I was out and drinking a fifth a day. Myrna went to the meetings, and then she went over to Mr Fixit's house to cook for him and clean up. His kids were no help in this regard. Nobody lifted a hand around Mr Fixit's house, except my wife when she was there.

All this happened not too long ago, three years about. It was something in those days.

I left my mother with the man on her sofa and drove around for a while. When I got home, Myrna made me a coffee.

She went out to the kitchen to do it while I waited until I heard her running water. Then I reached under a cushion for the bottle.

I think maybe Myrna really loved the man. But he also had a little something on the side – a twenty-two-year-old named Beverly. Mr Fixit did okay for a little guy who wore a button-up sweater.

He was in his mid-thirties when he went under. Lost his job and took up the bottle. I used to make fun of him when I had a chance. But I don't make fun of him anymore.

God bless and keep you, Mr Fixit.

He told Melody he'd worked on the moon shots. He told my daughter he was close friends with the astronauts. He told her he was going to introduce her to the astronauts as soon as they came to town.

It's a modern operation out there, the aerospace place where Mr Fixit used to work. I've seen it. Cafeteria lines, executive dining rooms, and the like. Mr Coffees in every office.

Mr Coffee and Mr Fixit.

Myrna says he was interested in astrology, auras, I Ching – that business. I don't doubt that this Ross was bright enough and interesting, like most of our ex-friends. I told Myrna I was sure she wouldn't have cared for him if he wasn't.

My dad died in his sleep, drunk, eight years ago. It was a Friday noon and he was fifty-four. He came home from work at the sawmill, took some sausage out of the freezer for his breakfast, and popped a quart of Four Roses.

My mother was there at the same kitchen table. She was trying to write a letter to her sister in Little Rock. Finally, my dad got up and went to bed. My mother said he never said good night. But it was morning, of course.

'Honey,' I said to Myrna the night she came home. 'Let's hug awhile and then you fix us a real nice supper.'

Myrna said, 'Wash your hands.'

CAL

From *Middlesex*

by Jeffrey Eugenides

Cal is an intersex man of Greek descent with a condition known as 5-alpha-reductase deficiency, which causes him to have certain feminine traits. He was brought up as a girl until puberty, and was called 'Callie'. Adult now, he feels that he has certain 'masculine' qualities and certain 'feminine' ones. This scene recounts a memory of when Cal was taken to Dr Luce's clinic as a teenager.

This character could be played by a man or by a masculine-presenting woman, or perhaps by a young androgynous-looking woman presenting as Callie at age fourteen, from the time of this memory.

In performance Cal might be holding the two key pieces of paper: the doctor's report and the 'coming out' letter to his parents. As he reads from the first, he is reacting to the revelations that it contains. Dr Luce's conclusion is shocking to him. This should be clear as he reads the report to us.

This memory marks a huge moment for the young Cal – when he finally realises, at age 14, what his identity is. The time is the mid-1970s. How you present yourself on stage will obviously have a significant impact on how this piece works in performance. If you are presenting as masculine then the opening passages will initially startle the audience; if you are presenting as feminine then there is a splendid defiance in the final lines.

Dr. Luce explained the estrogen injections would induce my breasts to grow. 'You won't be Raquel Welch, but you won't be Twiggy either.' My facial hair would diminish. My voice would rise from tenor to alto. But when I asked if I would finally get my period, Dr. Luce was frank. 'No. You won't. Ever. You won't be able to have a baby yourself,

Callie. If you want to have a family, you'll have to adopt.'

I received this news calmly. Having children wasn't something I thought about much at fourteen.

There was a knock on the door, and the receptionist stuck her head in. 'Sorry, Dr. Luce. But could I bother you a minute?'

'That depends on Callie.' He smiled at me. 'You mind taking a little break? I'll be right back.'

'I don't mind.'

'Sit there a few minutes and see if any other questions occur to you.' He left the room.

While he was gone, I didn't think of any other questions. I sat in my chair, not thinking anything at all. My mind was curiously blank. It was the blankness of obedience. With the unerring instinct of children, I had surmised what my parents wanted from me. They wanted me to stay the way I was. And this is what Dr. Luce now promised.

I was brought out of my abstracted state by a salmon-colored cloud passing low in the sky. I got up and went to the window to look out at the river. I pressed my cheek against the glass to see as far south as possible, where the skyscrapers rose. I told myself that I would live in New York when I grew up. 'This is the city for me,' I said. I had begun to cry again. I tried to stop. Dabbing at my eyes, I wandered around the office and finally found myself in front of one of the Mughal miniatures. In the small, ebony frame, two tiny figures were making love. Despite the exertion implied by their activity, their faces looked peaceful. Their expressions showed neither strain nor ecstasy. But of course the faces weren't the focal point. The geometry of the lovers' bodies, the graceful calligraphy of their limbs led the eye straight to the fact of their genitalia. The woman's pubic hair was a patch of evergreen against white snow, the man's member like a redwood sprouting from it. I looked. I looked once again to see how other people were made. As I looked, I didn't take sides. I understood both the urgency of the man and the pleasure of the woman. My mind was no longer blank. It was filled with dark knowledge.

I swung around. I wheeled and looked at Dr. Luce's desk. A file sat open there. He had left it when he hurried off.

PRELIMINARY STUDY: GENETIC XY (MALE) RAISED AS FEMALE

[...]

CONCLUSION

In speech, mannerisms, and dress, the subject manifests a feminine gender identity and role, despite a contrary chromosomal status.

It is clear by this that the sex of rearing, rather than genetic determinants, plays a greater role in the establishment of gender identity.

As the girl's gender identity was firmly established as female at the time her condition was discovered, a decision to implement feminizing surgery along with corresponding hormonal treatments seems correct. To leave the genitals as they are today would expose her to all manner of humiliation. Though it is possible that the surgery may result in partial or total loss of erotosexual satisfaction, sexual pleasure is only one factor in a happy life. The ability to marry and pass as a normal woman in society are also important goals, both of which will not be possible without feminizing surgery and hormone treatment. Also, it is hoped that new methods of surgery will minimize the effects of erotosexual dysfunction brought about by surgeries in the past, when feminizing surgery was in its infancy.

That evening, when my mother and I got back to the hotel, Milton [my dad] had a surprise. Tickets to a Broadway musical. I acted excited but later, after dinner, crawled into my parents' bed, claiming I was too tired to go.

'Too tired?' Milton said. 'What do you mean you're too tired?'

'That's okay, honey,' said Tessie [my mother]. 'You don't have to go.'

'Supposed to be a good show, Cal.'

'Is Ethel Merman in it?' I asked.

'No, smart-ass,' Milton said, smiling. 'Ethel Merman is not in it. She's not on Broadway right now. So we're seeing something with Carol Channing. She's pretty good, too. Why don't you come along?'

'No thanks,' I said.

'Okay, then. You're missing out.'

They started to go. 'Bye, honey,' my mother said.

Suddenly I jumped out of bed and ran to Tessie, hugging her.

'What's this for?' she asked.

My eyes brimmed with tears. Tessie took them to be tears of relief at everything we'd been through. In the narrow entryway carved from a former suite, cockeyed, dim, the two of us stood hugging and crying.

When they were gone, I got my suitcase from the closet. Then, looking at the turquoise flowers [on it], I exchanged it for my father's suitcase, a grey Samsonite. I left my skirts and my Fair Isle sweater in the dresser drawers. I packed only the darker garments, a blue crew neck, the alligator shirts, and my corduroys. The brassiere I abandoned, too. For the time being, I held on to my socks and panties, and I tossed in my toiletry case entire. When I was finished, I searched in Milton's garment bag for the cash he'd hidden there. The wad was fairly large and came to nearly three hundred dollars.

It wasn't all Dr. Luce's fault. I had lied to him about many things. His decision was based on false data. But he had been false in turn.

On a piece of stationery, I left a note for my parents.

> *Dear Mom and Dad,*
>
> *I know you're only trying to do what's best for me, but I don't think anyone knows for sure what's best. I love you and don't want to be a problem, so I've decided to go away. I know you'll say I'm not a problem, but I know I am. If you want to know why I'm doing this, you should ask Dr. Luce, who is a big liar! I am not a girl. I'm a boy. That's what I found out today. So I'm going where no one knows me. Everyone in Grosse Pointe will talk when they find out.*
>
> *Sorry I took your money, Dad, but I promise to pay you back someday, with interest.*
>
> *Please don't worry about me. I will be ALL RIGHT!*

Despite its content, I signed this declaration to my parents: 'Callie.'

It was the last time I was ever their daughter.

OLD WOMAN

From 'The Shed', in *Woman in a Lampshade* by Elizabeth Jolley

This is an edited version of the short story. The speaker is an old woman who lives alone on her farm. She may be holding the letter to which she refers, and reading from it when the time comes. She begins speaking directly to the audience but then gets distracted by her thoughts about the world of the farm, which the piece so vividly evokes. Perhaps she is deliberately distracting herself.

Perhaps she is standing just outside her farmhouse – referring in her shifts of attention to the physical reality she describes. You should try to evoke this world in your performance. The central theatrical tension in the piece is the contrast between her obsessive attention to the physical world of her house and the obvious undercurrent of terrible loneliness that she feels, alienated from her absent son. At first she seems to be scarcely aware of this, but obviously she feels it deeply.

Just outside the back door is a spongy patch of ground it sinks and rises whenever I step on and off it. There is something about it to be avoided, a place not to step on because of what might be underneath. Sometimes I think I'll get a spade and dig it up and then I think better not to in case there's something curled up there better left in peace. Perhaps it's something living or it might be something dead, buried there and the ground loose still under the matted surface roots of the grass. Of course there are bulbs in the ground, perhaps it is bulbs.

From down the slope below the vineyards and beyond my orchards comes the harsh voices of young cockatoos. Somewhere down there in the paperbarks and she-oaks there must be a nest. I never thought of black cockatoos as being young ever. To me they are always big birds full grown in screaming marauding flocks flying in masses arriving with their tremendous noise, unwelcome, staying only for what they want and then moving on. I never thought about the childhood of a cockatoo. Of course they have to come from somewhere. I never thought of them pausing in their destruction to make a nest and lay eggs.

I've just walked all the way up from the crossroads where I went to the store for onions and potatoes. There was a letter for me at the post office. I've fetched the letter too. I had to walk because there's something wrong with the mare and last week I had to leave the truck at the garage. It's stuck there down at the crossroads waiting for the delivery of a new battery. [...]

I'll keep my letter for later. I'm looking forward to it. It's from England. My son's over there. I hope it's from my son. When you're all alone in the bush you're not lonely really till you get a letter and then you want to read it straight away. You're hungry to read a letter it's nearly as good as having someone visit you. Writing a letter is good too, it's like being able to talk to someone, it's like talking to your son. It's my son I'd like to talk to most, I'd like to have him talk to me too. I'd like to hear his voice. [...]

Five miles is a long way to walk with potatoes but I had the letter to look forward to. The letter feels very thick so it must be long. The address is typed. I hope it's from my son. He's been in England a long time now. He's in a university teaching mathematics. [...]

I want to build a shed. I've had this shed in mind for years. I want a warm dry shed with space for tools and a trestle. I want it somewhere at the side of the house but not where it will block out the view from any one of the little windows. We built this weatherboard cottage years ago and made the windows so that we could look out on all sides of the place, into the bush and down over the crops and orchards to the mud flats of the creek. If anyone is approaching from any direction I can look out and see who is there. That's why I can't make up my mind exactly where to put the shed. I've got the timber. I've had it for years. I have to keep shifting it for if you leave wood standing too long in one place in this country, white ants get at it and reduce it to a kind of corrugated dirty cardboard. You can't build a shed with dust and earth. [...]

The letter must be from my boy, there's no one else to write to me from England. I'd like to open it at once but I'll keep it on the mantlepiece and open it a bit later on. I'll look forward to opening it. It's a long time since I had any news. He's not much of a letter writer. I suppose sums aren't like words. I've written to him. At one time I wrote every week telling him about the farm.

Since his marriage his wife writes at Christmas. I've got grown up grandchildren; they used to write at Christmas too but they've never seen me. I suppose I never seemed real to them.

Somewhere in the house I've got photographs of them all dressed up in coats and leggings going out to pick blackberries, and there's another with them all in party dresses sitting by their Christmas tree. I've stared at these photographs trying to see as much of them and their house as I can, trying to picture their lives. His wife, Kathryn, teaches in the university too, she always leans towards him in the photographs. It's a kind of possessive lean. She leans with her head a bit on one side, facing the camera and smiling and her body bent as if to say he belongs to her. Country women stand square beside their men as if planted and growing of themselves. [...]

Tonight when I'm resting I'll read the letter. Just now I'll think about the shed. I'll have a window on one side and double doors facing the west to catch the evening sun. A shed's a nice place to work in when the sun's coming in. [...]

All around my paddock the thieving goats are trying to get in. The top paddock is where they come and I've got my goat-watching chair up there. One night I fell asleep while waiting for the goats. When I woke up in the moonlight it seemed as if the trees had snow on them but it was the marri trees in flower, the creamy white clusters of flowers were tossed all over those great trees. It seemed as if my valley was dripping with honey and for days I could smell the honey.

Before I went down to the crossroads I tried to plough a bit above and below the cottage, but it's too dry and dusty. [...]

I'll go indoors and open the letter. It'll be like having my son home for a while. I want to read his letter, I want to know everything about him as I once did.

It's a typed letter. It's duplicated, copied by a machine. Someone has written 'Grandma' in ink next to the duplicated 'dear'. The letter is long, it starts as if it's from a lot of people:

'Dear Grandma once again it's time to catch the Christmas mail. We send you our warmest greetings and our best wishes for a happy Christmas and a good new year. The year has been a busy and eventful one for all of us. [...]

'Half way through the year our new home was finally completed and we moved and settled in, all of us coping with the necessary changes in our routine. As we are only six houses away from the shops Kathryn can shop daily and John can have the car without argument. The suburb is very attractive with Tudor houses and a fifteenth-century church.

'Shortly before moving Edwina announced her engagement and after graduating with honours she was quietly married and the buffet reception was held at a nearby hotel – '

Ah well, I suppose I'll have to read the rest of this, though there's nothing of him, no sound of his voice and no touch of his hand in it. It's all examination marks, interior decorating, food prices, holidays in the Alps with mushrooms included in the breakfasts, art galleries and picture galleries, museums and concerts. At the end his name is there with hers and the children's but the signatures are machine copies. It's like the noise of the cockatoos screeching their news. All these pages of successful academic activities, I keep seeing these dead words and no words for me, nothing I can get a hold of and see and feel. [...]

I'll go up to the old chair in the top paddock for a bit and watch them thieving goats. Starving goats can get through any kind of fence. I'll fix 'em tonight. Knowing the damage they do I'm surprised at anyone keeping goats. I'll fix 'em with pepper shot.

I can hear the cockatoos all the time. They've never stopped their screeching, a raucous gravelly noise like long big words that never stop. The parent birds must get to hate their young and yet continue to listen to them because there is no other way. How can a parent disregard the noise from the nest.

Perhaps the shed should be right outside the back door. Perhaps I should build it tomorrow over that spongy patch of ground. I could start tomorrow to level it off. If it's all bulbs there I won't know till the rains come. If there's something there to grow I'll see then whatever it is. Perhaps I'd better wait for the rains before I start to put up the shed and that gives me more time to think about it.

MOLLOY

From *Molloy*

by Samuel Beckett

This is a famous comic routine, in which the wandering vagrant Molloy explains at great length one of the pleasures he takes in life and also the extreme anxiety that it causes him. The text might look repetitive on the page but if you can get the warped logic right, and find the character, it is very funny. The end is very poignant, especially in the last lines' sudden dismissal of the whole problem.

The action of the piece is that Molloy really wants to explain his obsessive-compulsive interest in the details of his stone-sucking habit – like a drug addict obsessed with his kit. He is emotional about it, and connected with the physical reality – the stones in his mouth, the pockets of his coat and trousers. The theatrical journey is towards his discovery that he really doesn't need any of it. At the end he suddenly lets go of his obsession. The original routine is 2,500 words of unparagraphed text, which would take at least 30 minutes to perform. Here it is paragraphed and cut in half. You should read the entire routine, or look at one of the performances of it on YouTube, and work out the logic before you perform it.

There is great scope for theatricalising Molloy's explanations of his solution to his problem, using trousers, a coat and actions. He is delivering this straight to the audience. He really wants us to understand, at least until the end. You will have to make sure that they get it, and also reveal the fastidious character underneath. Don't play for laughs. If you play it for real it should be funny.

I took advantage of being at the seaside to lay in a store of sucking-stones. They were pebbles but I call them stones. Yes, on this occasion I laid in a considerable store. I distributed them equally between my four pockets, and sucked them turn and turn about. This raised a problem which I first solved in the following way. I had say sixteen stones, four in each of my four pockets these being the two pockets of my trousers and the two pockets of my greatcoat.

Taking a stone from the right pocket of my greatcoat, and putting it in my mouth, I replaced it in the right pocket of my greatcoat by a stone from the right pocket of my trousers, which I replaced by a stone from the left pocket of my trousers, which I replaced by a stone from the left pocket of my greatcoat, which I replaced by the stone which was in my mouth, as soon as I had finished sucking it.

Thus there were still four stones in each of my four pockets, but not quite the same stones. And when the desire to suck took hold of me again, I drew again on the right pocket of my greatcoat, certain of not taking the same stone as the last time. And while I sucked it I rearranged the other stones in the way I have just described. And so on.

But this solution did not satisfy me fully. For it did not escape me that, by an extraordinary hazard, the four stones circulating thus might always be the same four. In which case, far from sucking the sixteen stones turn and turn about, I was really only sucking four, always the same, turn and turn about. [...]

It was obvious that by increasing the number of my pockets I was bound to increase my chances of enjoying my stones in the way I planned, that is to say one after the other until their number was exhausted. Had I had eight pockets, for example, instead of the four I did have, then even the most diabolical hazard could not have prevented me from sucking at least eight of my sixteen stones, turn and turn about. The truth is I should have needed sixteen pockets in order to be quite easy in my mind. [...]

For I was beginning to lose all sense of measure, after all this wrestling and wrangling, and to say, All or nothing. And if I was tempted for an instant to establish a more equitable proportion between my stones and my pockets, by reducing the former to the number of the latter, it was only for an instant. For it would have been an admission of defeat. And sitting on the shore, before the sea, the sixteen stones spread out before my eyes, I gazed at them in anger and perplexity. [...]

Now I am willing to believe, indeed I firmly believe, that other solutions to this problem might have been found and indeed may still be found, no less sound, but much more elegant than the one I shall now describe, if

I can. And I believe too that had I been a little more insistent, a little more resistant, I could have found them myself. But I was tired, but I was tired, and I contented myself ingloriously with the first solution that was a solution, to this problem. But not to go over the heartbreaking stages through which I passed before I came to it here it is, in all its hideousness.

All (all!) that was necessary was to put, for example, to begin with, six stones in the right pocket of my greatcoat, or supply-pocket, five in the right pocket of my trousers, and five in the left pocket of my trousers, that makes the lot, twice five ten plus six sixteen, and none, for none remained, in the left pocket of my greatcoat, which for the time being remained empty, empty of stones that is, for its usual contents remained, as well as occasional objects. For where do you think I hid my vegetable knife, my silver, my horn and the other things that I have not yet named, perhaps shall never name. Good. Now I can begin to suck.

Watch me closely. I take a stone from the right pocket of my greatcoat, suck it, stop sucking it, put it in the left pocket of my greatcoat, the one empty (of stones). I take a second stone from the right pocket of my greatcoat, suck it, put it in the left pocket of my greatcoat. And so on until the right pocket of my greatcoat is empty (apart from its usual and casual contents) and the six stones I have just sucked, one after the other, are all in the left pocket of my greatcoat.

Pausing then, and concentrating, so as not to make a balls of it, I transfer to the right pocket of my greatcoat, in which there are no stones left, the five stones in the right pocket of my trousers, which I replace by the five stones in the left pocket of my trousers, which I replace by the six stones in the left pocket of my greatcoat. At this stage then the left pocket of my greatcoat is again empty of stones, while the right pocket of my greatcoat is again supplied, and in the right way, that is to say with other stones than those I have just sucked. These other stones I then begin to suck, one after the other, and to transfer as I go along to the left pocket of my greatcoat, being absolutely certain, as far as one can be in an affair of this kind, that I am not sucking the same stones as a moment before, but others. [...]

It was not enough to number the stones [as I could have done] for I would have had to remember, every time I put a stone in my mouth, the number I needed and look for it in my pocket. Which would have put me off stone for ever, in a very short time. For I would never have been sure of not making a mistake, unless of course I had kept a kind of register, in which to tick off the stones one by one, as I sucked them. And of this I believed myself incapable. No, the only perfect solution would have been the sixteen pockets, symmetrically disposed, each one with its stone. Then I would have needed neither to number nor to think, but merely, as I sucked a given stone, to move on the fifteen others, each to the next pocket, a delicate business admittedly, but within my power, and to call always on the same pocket when I felt like a suck. This would have freed me from all anxiety, not only within each cycle taken separately, but also for the sum of all cycles, though they went on forever. [...] But deep down I didn't give a tinker's curse about being off my balance, dragged to the right hand and the left, backwards and forwards. And deep down it was all the same to me whether I sucked a different stone each time or always the same stone, until the end of time. For they all tasted exactly the same. And if I had collected sixteen, it was not in order to ballast myself in such and such a way, or to suck them turn about, but simply to have a little store, so as never to be without.

But deep down I didn't give a fiddler's curse about being without, when they were all gone they would be all gone, I wouldn't be any the worse off, or hardly any. And the solution to which I rallied in the end was to throw away all the stones but one, which I kept now in one pocket, now in another, and which of course I soon lost, or threw away, or gave away, or swallowed.

ESTHER

From *The Bell Jar*

by Sylvia Plath

This is from a famous semi-autobiographical novel that has been loved for many reasons for many years. It is set in 1953: the narrator Esther Greenwood has just finished a stint in New York. She won a competition to guest edit a magazine there and the experience has disturbed her. She drops out of college and returns to live with her mother in Massachusetts. She decides to write a novel but quickly realises her lack of life experience. In this extract Esther imagines a number of scenarios for her future. Unable to keep her mind focused on one thing, she begins to read James Joyce's Finnegans Wake*, the most obscure novel ever written. Under the onslaught of this, her reading begins to blur and the letters in the texts she is trying to read start to transform.*

Working on this you need to decide how tough she is, underneath her negative feelings, and to what extent she is aware that something is coming loose in her mind. Your audience should understand, by her feverish anxiety, that she is becoming ill.

Some of the passages in italics are from the novel she is trying to write, and some are from Finnegans Wake*. She may be sitting at a desk, pounding away at an old-fashioned typewriter, then looking up at the audience, confiding in them. There is a fierce energy in her but also an underlying anxiety. There should be something defiant about her, but she also has emotional bruises.*

Elaine sat on the breezeway in an old yellow night-gown of her mother's, waiting for something to happen. It was a sweltering morning in July, and drops of sweat crawled down her back, one by one, like slow insects.

I leaned back and read what I had written. It seemed lively enough, and

I was quite proud of the bit about the drops of sweat like insects, only I had the dim impression I'd probably read it somewhere else a long time ago.

I sat like that for about an hour, trying to think what would come next, and in my mind, the barefoot doll in her mother's old yellow night-gown sat and stared into space as well.

'Why, honey, don't you want to get dressed'?

My mother took care never to tell me to do anything. She would only reason with me sweetly, like one intelligent, mature person with another.

'It's almost three in the afternoon.'

'I'm writing a novel,' I said. 'I haven't got time to change out of this and change into that.'

I lay on the couch on the breezeway and shut my eyes. I could hear my mother clearing the typewriter and the papers from the card-table and laying out the silver for supper, but I didn't move.

> *Inertia oozed like molasses through Elaine's limbs. That's what it must feel like to have malaria, she thought.*

At that rate, I'd be lucky if I wrote a page a day.

Then I knew what the trouble was.

I needed experience.

How could I write about life when I'd never had a love affair or a baby or seen anybody die? A girl I knew had just won a prize for a short story about her adventures among the pygmies in Africa. How could I compete with that sort of thing?

By the end of supper my mother had convinced me I should study shorthand in the evenings. Then I would be killing two birds with one stone, writing a novel and learning something practical as well. I would also be saving a whole lot of money.

That same evening, my mother unearthed an old blackboard from the cellar and set it up on the breezeway. Then she stood at the blackboard and scribbled little curlicues in white chalk while I sat in a chair and watched.

At first I felt hopeful.

I thought I might learn shorthand in no time, and when the freckled lady in the Scholarships Office asked me why I hadn't worked to earn money in July and August, the way you were supposed to if you were a scholarship girl, I could tell her I had taken a free shorthand course instead, so I could support myself right after college.

The only thing was, when I tried to picture myself in some job, briskly jotting down line after line of shorthand, my mind went blank. There wasn't one job I felt like doing where you used shorthand. And, as I sat there and watched, the white chalk curlicues blurred into senselessness.

I told my mother I had a terrible headache, and went to bed.

An hour later the door inched open, and she crept into the room. I heard the whisper of her clothes as she undressed. She climbed into bed. Then her breathing grew slow and regular.

In the dim light of the streetlamp that filtered through the drawn blinds, I could see the pin curls on her head glittering like a row of little bayonets.

I decided I would put off the novel until I had gone to Europe and had a lover, and that I would never learn a word of shorthand. If I never learned shorthand I would never have to use it.

I thought I would spend the summer reading *Finnegans Wake* and writing my thesis. Then I would be way ahead when college started at the end of September, and able to enjoy my last year instead of swotting away with no make-up and stringy hair, on a diet of coffee and benzedrine, the way most of the seniors taking honours did, until they finished their thesis.

Then I thought I might put off college for a year and apprentice myself to a pottery maker.

Or work my way to Germany and be a waitress, until I was bi-lingual.

Then plan after plan started leaping through my head, like a family of scatty rabbits.

I saw the years of my life spaced along a road in the form of telephone poles, threaded together by wires. I counted one, two, three ... nineteen telephone poles, and then the wires dangled into space, and try as I would I couldn't see a single pole beyond the nineteenth.

The room blued into view, and I wondered where the night had gone. My mother turned from a foggy log into a slumbering, middle-aged woman, her mouth slightly open and a snore ravelling from her throat. The piggish noise irritated me, and for a while it seemed to me that the only way to stop it would be to take the column of skin and sinew from which it rose and twist it to silence between my hands.

I feigned sleep until my mother left for school, but even my eyelids didn't shut out the light. They hung the raw, red screen of their tiny vessels in front of me like a wound. I crawled between the mattress and the padded bedstead and let the mattress fall across me like a tombstone. It felt dark and safe under there, but the mattress was not heavy enough.

It needed about a ton more weight to make me sleep.

> *riverrun, past Eve and Adam's, from swerve of shore to bend of bay, brings us by a commodious vicus of recirculation back to Howth Castle and Environs …*

The thick book made an unpleasant dent in my stomach.

> *riverrun, past Eve and Adam's…*

I thought the small letter at the start might mean that nothing ever really began all new, with a capital, but that it just flowed on from what came before. Eve and Adam's was Adam and Eve, of course, but it probably signified something else as well.

Maybe it was a pub in Dublin.

My eyes sank through an alphabet soup of letters to the long word in the middle of the page.

> *Bababadalgharaghtakamminarronnkonnbronntonnerronnruonn-thunntrovarrhounawnskawntoohoohoordenenthurnuk!*

I counted the letters. There were exactly a hundred of them.

I thought this must be important.

Why should there be a hundred letters?

Haltingly, I tried the word aloud.

It sounded like a heavy wooden object falling downstairs, boomp boomp boomp, step after step. Lifting the pages of the book, I let them fan slowly by my eyes. Words, dimly familiar but twisted all awry, like faces in a funhouse mirror, fled past, leaving no impression on the glassy surface of my brain.

I squinted at the page.

The letters grew barbs and rams' horns. I watched them separate, each from the other, and jiggle up and down in a silly way. Then they associated themselves in fantastic, untranslatable shapes, like Arabic or Chinese.

I decided to junk my thesis.

I decided to junk the whole honors program and become an ordinary English major. I went to look up the requirements of an ordinary English major at my college.

There were lots of requirements, and I didn't have half of them. One of the requirements was a course in the eighteenth century. I hated the very idea of the eighteenth century, with all those smug men writing tight little couplets and being so dead keen on reason. So I'd skipped it. They let you do that in honors, you were much freer. I had been so free I'd spent most of my time on Dylan Thomas.

A friend of mine, also in honors, had managed never to read a word of Shakespeare; but she was a real expert on the *Four Quartets.*

I saw how impossible and embarrassing it would be for me to try and switch from my free program into the stricter one. So I looked up the requirements for English majors at the city college where my mother taught.

They were even worse.

You had to know Old English and the History of the English language and a representative selection of all that had been written from Beowulf to the present day.

This surprised me. I had always looked down on my mother's college, as it was co-ed, and filled with people who couldn't get scholarships to the big eastern colleges.

Now I saw that the stupidest person at my mother's college knew more than I did. I saw they wouldn't even let me in through the door, let alone give me a large scholarship like the one I had at my own college.

I thought I had better go to work for a year and think things over. Maybe I could study the eighteenth century in secret.

But I didn't know shorthand, so what could I do?

I could be a waitress or a typist.

But I couldn't stand the idea of being either one.

'You say you want more sleeping pills?'

'Yes.'

'But the ones I gave you last week are very strong.'

'They don't work anymore.'

Teresa's large, dark eyes regarded me thoughtfully. I could hear the voices of her three children in the garden under the consulting-room window. My Aunt Libby had married an Italian, and Teresa was my aunt's sister-in-law and our family doctor.

I liked Teresa. She had a gentle, intuitive touch.

I thought it must be because she was Italian.

There was a little pause.

'What seems to be the matter?' Teresa said then.

'I can't sleep. I can't read.' I tried to speak in a cool, calm way, but the zombie rose up in my throat and choked me off. I turned my hands palms up.

'I think,' Teresa tore off a white slip from her prescription pad and wrote down a name and address, 'you'd better see another doctor I know. He'll be able to help you more than I can.' I peered at the writing but I couldn't read it.

'Doctor Gordon,' Teresa said. 'He's a psychiatrist.'

THE CHILD

From 'Children on a Country Road' by Franz Kafka

This is a complete short story, written in about 1910. It is a mysterious piece, very theatrical and full of joy. The identity of the speaker is unclear and so is open to performance choices, but the piece is a memory of a young child, probably (but not necessarily) a boy, playing by a road in a forest. It could be performed in many different ways. The experiences described are vividly those of a young child but the narrative voice sounds older and more reflective. There is the sudden transition from 'I' to 'one', when the child is lying in the ditch, when the speaker seems to be an older person looking back. The exuberance of the sudden bursts of shouted cries while the children are playing gives performance opportunities, as does the excitement of singing to the train. Perhaps you could actually sing at this point.

The ending seems abrupt until we realise that, at least in his or her imagination, the child has gone off on a big adventure, to another town where no-one gets tired and, perhaps, everyone has fun. Or perhaps the grown-up child has already done that, and found that in the city he or she is still yearning for the fun of the road.

I heard the wagons rumbling past the garden fence, sometimes I even saw them through gently swaying gaps in the foliage. How the wood of their spokes and shafts creaked in the summer heat! Laborers were coming from the fields and laughing so that it was a scandal.

I was sitting on our little swing, just resting among the trees in my parents' garden.

On the other side of the fence the traffic never stopped. Children's running feet were past in a moment; harvest wagons with men and women perched on and around the sheaves darkened the flower beds; toward evening I saw a gentleman slowly promenading with a walking stick, and a couple of girls who met him arm in arm stepped aside into the grass as they greeted him.

Then birds flew up as if in showers, I followed them with my eyes and saw how high they soared in one breath, till I felt not that they were rising but that I was falling, and holding fast to the ropes began to swing a little out of sheer weakness. Soon I was swinging more strongly as the air blew colder and instead of soaring birds trembling stars appeared.

I was given my supper by candlelight. Often both my arms were on the wooden board and I was already weary as I bit into my bread and butter. The coarse-mesh window curtains bellied in the warm wind and many a time some passer-by outside would stay them with his hands as if he wanted to see me better and speak to me. Usually the candle soon went out and in the sooty candle smoke the assembled midges went on circling for a while. If anyone asked me a question from the window I would gaze at him as if at a distant mountain or into vacancy, nor did he particularly care whether he got an answer or not. But if one jumped over the window sill and announced that the others were already waiting, then I did get to my feet with a sigh.

'What are you sighing for? What's wrong? Has something dreadful happened that can never be made good? Shan't we ever recover from it? Is everything lost?'

Nothing was lost. We ran to the front of the house. 'Thank God, here you are at last!' – 'You're always late!' – 'Why just me?' – 'Especially you, why don't you stay at home if you don't want to come.' – 'No quarter!' – 'No quarter? What kind of way is that to talk?'

We ran our heads full tilt into the evening. There was no daytime and no nighttime. Now our waistcoat buttons would be clacking together like teeth, again we would be keeping a steady distance from each other as we ran, breathing fire like wild beasts in the tropics. Like cuirassiers in old wars, stamping and springing high, we drove each other down the short alley and with this impetus in our legs a farther stretch along the main road. Stray figures went into the ditch, hardly had they vanished down the dusky escarpment when they were standing like newcomers on the field path above and looking down.

'Come on down!' – 'Come on up first!' – 'So's you can push us down, no thanks, we're not such fools.' – 'You're afraid, you mean. Come on up, you cowards!' – 'Afraid? Of the likes of you? You're going to push us down, are you? That's a good one.'

We made the attempt and were pushed head over heels into the grass of the roadside ditch, tumbling of our own free will. Everything was equably warm to us, we felt neither warmth nor chill in the grass, only one got tired.

Turning on one's right side, with a hand under the ear, one could easily have fallen asleep there. But one wanted to get up again with chin uplifted, only to roll into a deeper ditch. Then with an arm thrust out crosswise and legs threshing to the side one thought to launch into the air again only to fall for certain into a still deeper ditch. And of this one never wanted to make an end.

How one might stretch oneself out, especially in the knees, properly to sleep in the last ditch, was something scarcely thought of, and one simply lay on one's back, like an invalid, inclined to weep a little. One blinked as now and then a youngster with elbows pressed to his side sprang over one's head with dark-looming soles, in a leap from the escarpment to the roadway.

The moon was already some way up in the sky, in its light a mail coach drove past. A small wind began to blow everywhere, even in the ditch one could feel it, and nearby the forest began to rustle. Then one was no longer so anxious to be alone.

'Where are you?' – 'Come here!' – 'All together!' – 'What are you hiding for, drop your nonsense!' – 'Don't you know the mail's gone past already?' – 'Not already?' – 'Of course; it went past while you were sleeping.' – 'I wasn't sleeping. What an idea!' – 'Oh shut up, you're still half asleep.' – 'But I wasn't.' – 'Come on!'

We ran bunched more closely together, many of us linked hands, one's head could not be held high enough, for now the way was downhill. Someone whooped an Indian war cry, our legs galloped us as never before, the wind lifted our hips as we sprang. Nothing could have us; we were in such full stride that even in overtaking others we could fold our arms and look quietly around us.

At the bridge over the brook we came to a stop; those who had overrun it came back. The water below lapped against stones and roots as if it were not already late evening. There was no reason why one of us should not jump onto the parapet of the bridge.

From behind clumps of trees in the distance a railway train came past, all the carriages were lit up, the windowpanes were certainly let down. One of us began to sing a popular catch, but we all felt like singing. We sang much faster than the train was going, we waved our arms because our voices were not enough, our voices rushed together in an avalanche of sound that did us good. When one joins in song with others it is like being drawn on by a fish hook.

So we sang, the forest behind us, for the ears of the distant travelers. The grownups were still awake in the village, the mothers were making down the beds for the night.

Our time was up. I kissed the one next to me, reached hands to the three nearest, and began to run home, none called me back. At the first crossroads where they could no longer see me I turned off and ran by the field paths into the forest again. I was making for that city in the south of which it was said in our village:

'There you'll find queer folk! Just think, they never sleep!'

'And why not?'

'Because they never get tired.'

'And why not?'

'Because they're fools.'

'Don't fools get tired?'

'How could fools get tired!'

VIVIEN

From 'Amundsen', in *Dear Life* by Alice Munro

Vivien is a young schoolteacher working in a tuberculosis sanatorium in the forest outside Toronto, Canada, towards the end of World War II. She is an intelligent and well-read young woman from the city who finds herself in this isolated and lonely place. Alister is the doctor in the sanatorium. In the original short story it's clear that he is a sexual predator who had no real intention of marrying her but this extract reveals his true nature gradually. Vivien probably had an inkling of the truth but at first, as you can see, she clings to her illusion. In all the little details we can see what she can't.

The challenge in performance is to keep the audience guessing and to play both her inkling and her illusion at the same time. As she tells this sad little story the realisation dawns on her but even at the end (at least in the short story – in performance you could play it another way) she clings to her hope. How you play what she does after the final line will tell us a lot about her.

In the short story most of it is narrated in the past tense, from a perspective later in life, but you don't have to play it this way. The tense switches in this extract to the present, as she vividly recalls this one crucial scene in her life, when she was first betrayed.

We are going to Huntsville.

Going to Huntsville – our code for getting married.

We have begun the day that I am sure I will remember all my life. I have my green crepe dry-cleaned and rolled up carefully in my overnight bag. My grandmother once taught me the trick of tight rolling, so much better than folding to prevent wrinkles. I suppose I will have to change my clothes in a ladies' toilet somewhere. I am watching to see if there are any early wildflowers along the road, that I could pick to make a bouquet. Would he agree to my having a bouquet? But it's too early even for marsh marigolds. Along the empty curving road nothing is to be seen but skinny black spruce trees and islands of spreading juniper and bogs. And in the road cuts a chaotic jumble of the rocks that have become familiar to me here – bloodstained iron and slanting shelves of granite.

The car radio is on and playing triumphal music, because the Allies are getting closer and closer to Berlin. The doctor – Alister – says that they are delaying to let the Russians in first. He says they'll be sorry.

Now that we are away from Amundsen I find that I can call him Alister. This is the longest drive we have ever taken together and I am aroused by his male unawareness of me – which I know now can quickly shift to its opposite – and by his casual skill as a driver. I find it exciting that he is a surgeon though I would never admit that. Right now I believe I could lie down for him in any bog or mucky hole, or feel my spine crushed against any roadside rock, should he require an upright encounter. I know too that I must keep these feelings to myself.

I turn my mind to the future. Once we get to Huntsville I expect that we will find a minister and stand side by side in a living room which will have some of the modest gentility of my grandparents' apartment, of the living rooms I have known all my life. I recall times when my grandfather would be sought out for wedding purposes even after his retirement. My grandmother would rub a little rouge on her cheeks and take out the dark blue lace jacket that she kept for being a witness on such occasions.

But I discover there are other ways to get married, and another aversion of my bridegroom's that I hadn't grasped. He won't have anything to do with a minister. In the Town Hall in Huntsville we fill out forms that swear to our single state and make an appointment to be married by a justice of the peace later in the day.

Time for lunch. Alister stops outside a restaurant that could be a first cousin to the coffee shop in Amundsen.

'This'll do?'

But on looking into my face he does change his mind.

'No?' he says. 'Okay.'

We end up eating lunch in the chilly front room of one of the genteel houses that advertise chicken dinners. The plates are icy cold, there are no other diners, there is no radio music but only the clink our cutlery as we try to separate parts of the stringy chicken. I am sure he is thinking that we might have done better in the restaurant he suggested in the first place.

Nonetheless I have the courage to ask about the ladies' room, and there, in cold air even more discouraging than that of the front room, I shake out my green dress and put it on, repaint my mouth and fix my hair.

When I come out Alister stands up to greet me and smiles and squeezes my hand and says I look pretty.

We walk stiffly back to the car, holding hands. He opens the car door for me, goes round and gets in, settles himself and turns the key in the ignition, then turns it off.

The car is parked in front of a hardware store. Shovels for snow removal are on sale at half price. There is still a sign in the window that says skates can be sharpened inside.

Across the street there is a wooden house painted an oily yellow. Its front steps have become unsafe and two boards forming an *X* have been nailed across them.

The truck parked in front of Alister's car is a prewar model, with a runningboard and a fringe of rust on its fenders. A man in overalls comes out of the hardware store and gets into it. After some engine complaint, then some rattling and bouncing in place, it is driven away. Now a delivery truck with the store's name on it tries to park in the space left vacant. There is not quite enough room. The driver gets out and comes and raps on Alister's window. Alister is surprised – if he had not been talking so earnestly he would have noticed the problem. He rolls down the window and the man asks if we are parked there because we intend to buy something in the store. If not, could we please move along?

'Just leaving,' says Alister, the man sitting beside me who was going to marry me but now is not going to marry me.

'We were just leaving.'

We. He has said we. For a moment I cling to that word. Then I think it's the last time. The last time I'll be included in his we.

It's not the 'we' that matters, that is not what tells me the truth. It's his male-to-male tone to the driver, his calm and reasonable apology. I could wish now to go back to what he was saying before, when he did not even notice the van trying to park. What he was saying then had been terrible but his tight grip on the wheel, his grip and his abstraction and his voice had pain in them. No matter what he said and meant, he spoke out of the same deep place then, that he spoke from when he was in bed with me. But it is not so now, after he has spoken to another man. He rolls up the window and gives his attention to the car, to backing it out of its tight spot and moving it so as not to come in contact with the van.

And a moment later I would be glad even to go back to that time, when he craned his head to see behind him. Better that than driving – as he is driving now – down the main street of Huntsville, as if there is no more to be said or managed.

I can't do it, he has said.

He has said that he can't go through with this.

He can't explain it.

Only that it's a mistake.

I think that I will never be able to look at curly *S*'s like those on the Skates Sharpened sign, without hearing his voice. Or at rough boards knocked into an *X* like those across the steps of the yellow house opposite the store.

'I'm going to drive you to the station now. I'll buy your ticket to Toronto. I'm pretty sure there's a train to Toronto late in the afternoon. I'll think up some very plausible story and I'll get somebody to pack up your things. You'll need to give me your Toronto address, I don't think I've kept it. Oh, and I'll write you a reference. You've done a good job. You wouldn't have finished out a term anyway – I hadn't told you yet but the children are going to be moved. All kinds of big changes going on.'

A new tone in his voice, almost jaunty. A knockabout tone of relief. He is trying to hold that in, not let relief out till I am gone.

I watch the streets. It's something like being driven to the place of execution. Not yet. A little while yet. Not yet do I hear his voice for the last time. Not yet.

He doesn't have to ask the way. I wonder out loud if he has put girls on the train before.

'Don't be like that,' he says.

Every turn is like a shearing-off of what's left of my life.

There is a train to Toronto at five o'clock. He has told me to wait in the car, while he goes in to check. He comes out with the ticket in his hand and what I think is a lighter step. He must have realized this because as he approaches the car he becomes more sedate.

'It's nice and warm in the station. There's a special ladies' waiting room.'

He has opened the car door for me.

'Or would you rather I waited and saw you off? Maybe there's a place where we can get a decent piece of pie. That was a horrible dinner.'

This makes me stir myself. I get out and walk ahead of him into the station. He points out the ladies' waiting room. He raises an eyebrow at me and tries to make a final joke.

'Maybe someday you'll count this one of the luckiest days of your life.'

FELIX

From *Once*

by Morris Gleitzman

Felix, a young Jewish boy, is placed in a Catholic orphanage by his parents while they try to continue their book-selling business in Nazi-occupied Poland. This extract is from the first chapter in Gleitzman's book. It quickly establishes Felix as a resourceful youngster and a caring friend trying to make the most of his suddenly terrible situation.

The central theatrical tension here is between his boyish innocence and the new world that he has been placed in. He has little understanding of where he is. During the course of this piece he discovers some strength but at the end he still doesn't seem to realise that he is surely now an orphan.

Once I was living in an orphanage in the mountains and I shouldn't have been and I almost caused a riot.

It was because of the carrot.

You know how when a nun serves you very hot soup from a big metal pot and she makes you lean in close so she doesn't drip and the steam from the pot makes your glasses go all misty and you can't wipe them because you're holding your dinner bowl and the fog doesn't clear even when you pray to God, Jesus, the Virgin Mary, the pope and Adolf Hitler?

That's happening to me.

Somehow I find my way towards my table. I use my ears for navigation.

Dodie who always sits next to me is a loud slurper because of his crooked teeth. I hold my bowl above my head so other kids can't pinch my soup while I'm fogged up and I use Dodie's slurping noises to guide me in.

I feel for the edge of the table and put my bowl down and wipe my glasses.

That's when I see the carrot.

It's floating in my soup, huge among the flecks of cabbage and the tiny blobs of pork fat and the few lonely lentils and the bits of grey plaster from the kitchen ceiling.

A whole carrot.

I can't believe it. Three years and eight months I've been in this orphanage and I haven't had a whole carrot in my dinner bowl once. Neither has anyone else. Even the nuns don't get whole carrots, and they get bigger serving than us kids because they need the extra energy for being holy.

We can't grow vegetables up here in the mountains. Not even if we pray a lot. It's because of the frosts. So if a whole carrot turns up in this place, first it gets admired, then it gets chopped into enough pieces so that sixty-two kids, eleven nuns and one priest can all have a bit.

I stare at the carrot.

At this moment I'm probably the only kid in Poland with a whole carrot in his dinner bowl. For a few seconds I think it's a miracle. Except it can't be because miracles only happened in ancient times and this is 1942.

Then I realise what the carrot means and I have to sit down quick before my legs give way.

I can't believe it.

At last. Thank you God, Jesus, Mary, the Pope and Adolf Hitler, I've waited so long for this.

It's a sign.

This carrot is a sign from Mum and Dad. They've sent my favourite vegetable to let me know their problems are finally over. To let me know that after three long years and eight long months things are finally improving for Jewish booksellers. To let me know they're coming to take me home.

Yes.

Dizzy with excitement, I stick my fingers into the soup and grab the carrot.

Luckily the other kids are concentrating on their own dinners, spooning their soup up hungrily and peering into their bowls in case there's a speck of meat there, or a speck of rat poo.

I have to move fast.

If the others see my carrot there'll be a jealousy riot.

This is an orphanage. Everyone here is meant to have dead parents. If the other kids find out mine aren't dead, they'll get really upset and the nuns here could be in trouble with the Catholic head office in Warsaw for breaking the rules.

'Felix Saint Stanislaus.'

I almost drop the carrot. It's Mother Minka's voice, booming at me from the high table.

Everyone looks up.

'Don't fiddle with your food, Felix,' says Mother Minka. 'If you've found an insect in your bowl, just eat it and be grateful.'

The other kids are all staring at me. Some are grinning. Others are frowning and wondering what's going on. I try not to look like a kid who's just slipped a carrot into his pocket. I'm so happy I don't care that my fingers are stinging from the hot soup.

Mum and Dad are coming at last.

They must be down in the village. They must have sent the carrot up here with Father Ludwik to surprise me.

When everyone has gone back to eating, I give Mother Minka a grateful smile. It was good of her to make a joke to draw attention away from my carrot.

There were two reasons Mum and Dad chose this orphanage, because it was the closest and because of Mother Minka's goodness. When they were bringing me here, they told me how in all the years Mother Minka was a customer of their bookshop, back before things got difficult for Jewish booksellers, she never once criticised a single book.

Mother Minka doesn't see my smile, she's too busy glaring at the Saint Kazimierz table, so I give Sister Elwira a grateful smile too. Sister Elwira doesn't notice either because she's too busy serving the last few kids and being sympathetic to a girl who's crying about the amount of ceiling plaster in her soup.

They're so kind, these nuns. I'll miss them when Mum and Dad take me home and I stop being Catholic and go back to being Jewish.

'Don't you want that?' says a voice next to me.

Dodie is staring at my bowl. His is empty. He's sucking his teeth and I can see he's hoping my soup is up for grabs.

Over his shoulder, Marek and Telek are sneering.

'Grow up, Dodek,' says Marek, but in his eyes there's a flicker of hope that he might get some too.

Part of me wants to give up my soup to Dodie because his mum and dad died of sickness when he was three. But these are hard times and food is scarce and even when your tummy's stuffed with joy you still have to force it down.

I force it down.

Dodie grins. He knew I'd want it. The idea that I wouldn't is so crazy it makes us both chuckle.

Then I stop. I'll have to say goodbye to everyone here soon. That makes me feel sad. And when the other kids see Mum and Dad are alive, they'll know I haven't been truthful with them. That makes me feel even sadder.

I tell myself not to be silly. It's not like they're my friends, not really. You can't have friends when you're leading a secret life. With friends you might get too relaxed and blurt stuff out and then they'll know you've just been telling them a story.

But Dodie feels like my friend.

While I finish my soup I try to think of a good thing I can do for him. Something to show him I'm glad I know him. Something to make his life here a bit better after I've gone, after I'm back in my own home with my own books and my own mum and dad.

I know exactly what I can do for Dodie.

Now's the moment. The bath selection has just started.

Mother Minka is standing at the front, checking Jozef all over for dirt. He's shivering. We're all shivering. The bathroom is freezing, even now in summer. Probably because it's so big and below ground level. In ancient times, when this convent was first built, this bathroom was probably used for ice-skating.

Mother Minka flicks her tassel towards the dormitory. Jozef grabs his clothes and hurries away, relieved.

'Lucky pig,' shivers Dodie.

I step out of the queue and go up to Mother Minka.

'Excuse me, Mother,' I say.

She doesn't seem to notice me. She's peering hard as Borys, who's got half the playing field under his fingernails and toenails. And a fair bit of it in his armpits. I can see Mother Minka is about to flick her tassel towards the bath.

Oh no, I'm almost too late.

Then Mother Minka turns to me.

'What is it?' she says.

'Please, Mother,' I say hurriedly. 'Can Dodek be first in the bath?'

The boys behind me in the queue start muttering. I don't glance back at Dodie. I know he'll understand what I'm trying to do.

'Why?' says Mother Minka.

I step closer. This is between me and Mother Minka.

'You know how Dodek's parents died of sickness,' I say. 'Well Dodek's decided he wants to be a doctor and devote his life to wiping out sickness all over the world. The thing is, as a future doctor he's got to get used to being really hygienic and washing himself in really hot and clean water.'

I hold my breath and hope Dodie didn't hear me. He actually wants to be a pig-slaughterer and I'm worried he might say something.

Mother Minka looks at me.

'Get to the back of the queue,' she says.

'He really needs to be first in the bath every week,' I say. 'As a doctor.'

'Now,' booms Mother Minka.

I don't argue. You don't with Mother Minka. Nuns can have good hearts and still be violent.

As I pass Dodie he gives me a grateful look. I give him an apologetic one. I know he wouldn't mind about the doctor stories. He likes my stories. Plus I think he'd be a good doctor. Once, after he pulled the legs off a fly, he managed to stick a couple back on.

Ow, this stone floor is really cold on bare feet. That's something Dodie could do in the future. Design bathroom heating systems. I bet by the year 2000 every bathroom in the world will be heated. Floors and everything. With robots to pick the twigs and grit out of the bathwater.

Look at that, Borys is the first one in and the water's brown already. I can imagine what it'll be like when I finally get in. Cold, with more solid bits in it than our soup.

I close my eyes and think about the baths Mum and Dad used to give me. In front of the fire with clean water and lots of warm wet cuddles and lots and lots of stories.

I can't wait to have a bath like that again.

Hurry up, Mum and Dad.

JOHN BARTLE

From *The Yellow Birds*

by Kevin Powers

John Bartle is a returned soldier who served as a sniper with the American army during the invasion of Iraq. He had a friend called Daniel Murphy, whom we learn at the beginning of this extract has been killed. John is suffering from PTSD and at the climax of the book, from which this speech is taken, we learn exactly what it is that haunts him. Sterling is his Sergeant. John is talking partly to the audience, trying to explain himself, but he also sometimes gets lost in the vividness of his memory.

The setting should indicate some of this. In the book, he is now living in a derelict apartment, in a terrible state of personal neglect. There is a photo of Murphy, as a young man with a girlfriend, on the wall, with John's medals pinned next to it, and other military memorabilia. He is probably smoking and there may be empty beer bottles spread around.

Daniel Murphy was dead.

'Not so high up, if you really think about,' Sterling said.

'What?'

'I think he was probably dead before he fell. It just isn't that great a height.'

It was truly not a fall from all that great a height: broken bones were broken further, no resistance or attempt to land was made; the body had fallen, the boy already dead, the fall itself meaning nothing.

We pulled Murph free from the tangle of brush and laid him out in some shadow of respectability. We stood and looked him over. He was broken and bruised and cut and still pale except for his face and hands, and now his eyes had been gouged out, the two hollow sockets looking like red angry passages to his mind. His throat had been cut nearly through, his head hung limply and lolled from side to side, attached only by the barely intact vertebrae. We dragged him like a shot deer out of the wood line, trying but failing to keep his naked body from banging against the hard ground and bouncing in a way that would be forever burned into our memories. His ears were cut off. His nose cut off, too. He had been imprecisely castrated.

He'd been with us for ten months. He was eighteen years old. Now he was anonymous. The picture of him that would appear in the newspaper would be of him in Class A's in basic, a few pimples on his chin. We'd never be able to see him that way again.

I took my woobie out of my pack and covered him. I couldn't look any more. Most of us had seen death in many forms: the slick mess after a suicide bomber, headless bodies gathered in a ditch like a collection of broken dolls on a child's shelf, even our own boys sometimes, bleeding and crying as it became apparent that the sound of a casevac was thirty seconds too far in the distance. But none of us had seen this.

'What should we do with him?' I asked. The words themselves seemed incomprehensible. I drifted in and around the significance of the question, first reckoning with the fact that the decision would be ours. Two boys, one twenty-four, the other twenty-one, would decide what should happen to the body of a boy who had died and been butchered in the service of his country in an unknown corner of the world.

We knew that if we brought him back, there would be questions. Who found him? What did he look like? What was it like?

'Fuck, little man. You didn't have to go out like this,' Sterling said to the body at his feet. He flopped down on his butt into the dry grass and took his helmet off.

I sat next to Murph and began to tremble, rocking back and forth.

'You know what we got to do.'

'Not like this, Sarge.'

'It's what we do. No matter what. You know that shit, Bart.'

'It'll be worse.'

'We don't decide. That's way above our pay grade.'

'Sarge, you gotta trust me. We can't let that happen.'

We both knew what that was. There are few real mysteries in life. The body would be flown to Kuwait, where it would be mended and embalmed as best it could by mortuary affairs. It would land in Germany, tucked into a stack of plain metal caskets as the plane refueled. It would land in Dover, and someone would receive it, with a flag, and the thanks of a grateful nation, and in a moment of weakness his mother would turn up the lid of the casket and see her son, Daniel Murphy, see what had been done to him, and he would be buried and forgotten by all but her, as she sat alone in her rocking chair in the Appalachians long into every evening, forgetting herself, no longer bathing, no longer sleeping, the ashes of the cigarettes she smoked becoming long and seeming always about to fall to her feet. And we'd remember too, because we would have had the chance to change it.

He stood up and started pacing. 'Let's just think this through a minute,' he said. 'Let me get a smoke.'

I gave him one and lit one for myself. My hands were shaking and my lighter wouldn't stay lit in the wind and the wind blew the woobie and uncovered what was left of Murph's face. Sterling stared at the empty sockets. I put the blanket back. Minutes ticked into the past. A few birds darted in and out of the brush and sang. The sound of the river became clearer.

'You better not be wrong about this.'

I couldn't think. I wanted to take it all back. 'This is so fucked, Sarge.'

'Chill out, man. Just chill out, all right,' he said, and then paused reflectively. 'Here's what we do: you get on that radio and tell the terp to send over the hajji with the cart. Tell them we didn't find him.'

I took a minute and collected myself. Sterling went on, 'We're gonna have to fix this like it never happened. You know what that means, right?'

'Yeah. I know.'

'You sure?'

'I'm sure.'

We waited. A strange peace took shape between us. The sun muted the periphery into a mere abstraction of color and shape. Everything we did not look at directly became a blur in the corners of our eyes. We watched the hermit come, tapping lightly at the haunch of his mule. He walked slowly in the heat and all that was clear in our vision was the man and his lame mule emerging out of a hazy mirage, everything else vague or inverted or duplicate. The mule treaded lightly on its tinkered foreleg, and the man patiently guided it toward us. As he came closer we saw that the two mutts from before loped along behind him. The hermit approached and looked each of us in the eye as if we were lined up for an open-rank inspection, and finally said, 'Give me a cigarette, mister.' I gave him one and he lit it, inhaled deeply and smiled.

Sterling reached for Murph's legs and tried to lift him up. We didn't have the chance to take it back. We had never had the chance, not really. It was as if we had already done it in another life I could only vaguely remember. The decision had been made. I moved to where Sterling was and grabbed Murph by the arms. I shuddered quickly. My heart beat recklessly. We picked Murph up and brushed the dancing flies from his skin and tried not to look into his empty sockets as we laid him in the back of the cart among the clay and stone and the figurines of straw.

'We'll take him to the river,' Sterling said. 'We'll leave him there. Give me your lighter, Bart.'

I did. He lit the Zippo and left it burning and dropped it into the dry brush at the base of the tower.

'Let's go,' he said.

It was not far from the river, and we walked behind the hermit as he led the mule into some approximation of a trot. We followed behind this odd coterie of man and mule and dog for a half a klick or so, until we saw the banks of the river. Water lapped the edges and bulrushes swayed gently in the shallows at the banks.

Sterling tapped on my shoulder, pointed behind me, and I saw the minaret in flames from the dried brush burning at its base. Burn it. Burn the motherfucker down. The tower lit up like a flickering candle as the sun began to descend from its brutal apex. I thought for a moment that we might burn down the whole city for that one tower. I was briefly ashamed, and quickly forgot why.

Sterling looked at me and whispered, mostly to himself, 'Fuck 'em, man. Fuck everyone on earth.'

EVE

From Eve's Diary

by Mark Twain

This is an edited extract from an imagined diary of Eve, first published in the 1905 Christmas edition of Harper's Bazaar. *Twain imagines what Eve might have written, had she been recording her thoughts when she first came into the world as a fully-formed woman with no childhood. Twain is satirising the biblical story, and also the relationships between women and men as he saw them when he wrote it, but to play this you might have to capture her innocence in an ironic way. In performance, perhaps she is being disingenuous, pretending innocence.*

Saturday. – I am almost a whole day old, now. I arrived yesterday. That is as it seems to me. And it must be so, for if there was a day-before-yesterday I was not there when it happened, or I should remember it. It could be, of course, that it did happen, and that I was not noticing. Very well; I will be very watchful now, and if any day-before-yesterdays happen I will make a note of it. It will be best to start right and not let the record get confused, for some instinct tells me that these details are going to be important to the historian some day. For I feel like an experiment, I feel exactly like an experiment; it would be impossible for a person to feel more like an experiment than I do, and so I am coming to feel convinced that that is what I am – an experiment; just an experiment, and nothing more.

Then if I am an experiment, am I the whole of it? No, I think not; I think the rest of it is part of it. I am the main part of it, but I think the rest of it has its share in the matter. Is my position assured, or do I have to watch it and take care of it? The latter, perhaps. Some instinct tells me that eternal vigilance is the price of supremacy. (That is a good phrase, I think, for one so young.)

Everything looks better today than it did yesterday. In the rush of finishing up yesterday, the mountains were left in a ragged condition, and some of the plains were so cluttered with rubbish and remnants that the aspects were quite distressing. Noble and beautiful works of art should not be subjected to haste; and this majestic new world is indeed a most noble and beautiful work. And certainly marvellously near to being perfect, notwithstanding the shortness of the time. There are too many stars in some places and not enough in others, but that can be remedied presently, no doubt. The moon got loose last night, and slid down and fell out of the scheme – a very great loss; it breaks my heart to think of it. There isn't another thing among the ornaments and decorations that is comparable to it for beauty and finish. It should have been fastened better. If we can only get it back again – But of course there is no telling where it went to. And besides, whoever gets it will hide it; I know it because I would do it myself. I believe I can be honest in all other matters, but I already begin to realize that the core and centre of my nature is love of the beautiful, a passion for the beautiful, and that it would not be safe to trust me with a moon that belonged to another person and that person didn't know I had it. I could give up a moon that I found in the daytime, because I should be afraid someone was looking; but if I found it in the dark, I am sure I should find some kind of an excuse for not saying anything about it. For I do love moons, they are so pretty and so romantic. I wish we had five or six; I would never go to bed; I should never get tired lying on the moss-bank and looking up at them.

Stars are good, too. I wish I could get some to put in my hair. But I suppose I never can. You would be surprised to find how far off they are, for they do not look it. When they first showed, last night, I tried to knock some down with a pole, but it didn't reach, which astonished me; then I tried clods till I was all tired out, but I never got one. It was because I am left-handed and cannot throw good. Even when I aimed at the one I wasn't after I couldn't hit the other one, though I did make some close shots, for I saw the black blot of the clod sail right into the midst of the golden clusters forty or fifty times, just barely missing them, and if I could have held out a little longer maybe I could have got one.

So I cried a little, which was natural, I suppose, for one of my age, and after I was rested I got a basket and started for a place on the extreme rim of the circle, where the stars were close to the ground and I could get them with my hands, which would be better, anyway, because I could gather them tenderly then, and not break them. But it was farther than I thought, and at last I had to give it up; I was so tired I couldn't drag my feet another step; and besides, they were sore and hurt me very much.

I couldn't get back home; it was too far and turning cold; but I found some tigers and nestled in among them and was most adorably comfortable, and their breath was sweet and pleasant, because they live on strawberries. I had never seen a tiger before, but I knew them in a minute by the stripes. If I could have one of those skins, it would make a lovely gown.

Today I am getting better about distances. I was so eager to get hold of every pretty thing that I giddily grabbed for it, sometimes when it was too far off, and sometimes when it was but six inches away but seemed a foot – alas, with thorns between! I learned a lesson; also I made an axiom, all out of my own head – my very first one; *the scratched experiment shuns the thorn*. I think it is a very good one for one so young.

I followed the other Experiment around, yesterday afternoon, at a distance, to see what it might be for, if I could. But I was not able to make out. I think it is a man. I had never seen a man, but it looked like one, and I feel sure that that is what it is. I realized that I feel more curiosity about it than about any of the other reptiles. If it is a reptile, and I suppose it is; for it has frowzy hair and blue eyes, and looks like a reptile. It has no hips; it tapers like a carrot; when it stands, it spreads itself apart like a derrick; so I think it is a reptile, though it may be architecture.

I was afraid of it at first, and started to run every time it turned around, for I thought it was going to chase me; but by and by I found it was only trying to get away, so after that I was not timid any more, but tracked it along, several hours, about twenty yards behind, which made it nervous and unhappy. At last it was a good deal worried, and climbed a tree. I waited a good while, then gave it up and went home.

Today the same thing over. I've got it up the tree again.

Sunday. – It is up there yet. Resting, apparently. But that is a subterfuge: Sunday isn't the day of rest, Saturday is appointed for that. It looks to me like a creature that is more interested in resting than in anything else. It would tire me to rest so much. It tires me just to sit around and watch the tree. I do wonder what it is for; I never see it do anything.

They returned the moon last night, and I was *so* happy! I think it is very honest of them. It slid down and fell off again, but I was not distressed; there is no need to worry when one has that kind of neighbours; they will fetch it back. I wish I could do something to show my appreciation. I would like to send them some stars, for we have more than we can use. I mean I, not we, for I can see that the reptile cares nothing for such things.

It has low tastes, and is not kind. When I went there yesterday evening in the gloaming it had crept down and was trying to catch the little speckled fishes that play in the pool, and I had to clod it to make it go up the tree again and let them alone. I wonder if *that* is what it is for? Hasn't it any heart? Hasn't it any compassion for those little creatures? Can it be that it was designed and manufactured for such ungentle work? It has the look of it. One of the clods took it back of the ear, and it used language. It gave me a thrill, for it was the first time I had ever heard speech, except my own. I did not understand the words, but they seemed expressive. [...]

By watching, I know that the stars are not going to last. I have seen some of the best ones melt and run down the sky. Since one can melt, they all can melt; since they can all melt, they can all melt the same Night. That sorrow will come – I know it. I mean to sit up every night and look at them as long as I can keep awake; and I will impress those sparkling fields on my memory, so that by and by when they are taken away I can by my fancy restore those lovely myriads to the black sky and make them sparkle again, and double them by the blur of my tears.

NATAN

From *The Secret Chord*

by Geraldine Brooks

The book is a fictional account of the life of the biblical King David. Natan is the prophet Nathan. Schlomo is the young King Solomon, son of David. Mitzrayim is Egypt, adjacent to the united kingdom of Judea and Israel over which David rules. These are hugely important figures in the theologies of Judaism, Christianity and Islam. Obviously you cannot play all this but it should inform your performance of this otherwise simple human piece.

Natan is a middle-aged man who has never had a family. He has served his king well as a prophet and counsellor, and in this piece he shows his pleasure at being allowed to become the tutor of his king's young son, Schlomo. The boy is five.

You will need to create three distinct voices to make this scene work. At first Natan tells his story from the perspective of an old man recalling his past, but as the piece develops he becomes increasingly immersed in his younger self, interacting excitedly with the king's son. Underlying this is Natan's joy in the fact that he knows, from a vision, that the boy will one day become king, pushing out his older brothers Amnon and Avshalom, about whom he is so anxious in this extract. Towards the end Natan hints at this vision, and there is suddenly something like a quiet complicity between him and the boy.

The title of the novel is taken from Leonard Cohen's famous song, 'Hallelujah'. You could use the first few bars of this to set the scene of your performance.

You could say he found his own way to me. That is how it would have seemed, to any who did not know better. A psalmist might fashion it otherwise. Such a one would say he was carried to me on the wings of an eagle.

There had been a great storm in the night, lashing rains and high winds such as we rarely see in these hills. In the morning, the winds had died, but the rain continued to fall steadily, filling the dry wadis till they brimmed, spilling between the rocks in the swift freshets. It was a day to be spent indoors, by the fire with the shutters closed. Not a day to expect guests.

Muwat, who was cleaning my armour – which was, happily, tarnished from disuse – flinched in surprise at the heavy rapping on the outer gate. He flung a shawl over his head and went out.

The boy did not wait to be announced, but burst in, wet through, his attendant – a tall, thin Mitzrayimite – hunched sodden and miserable behind him. He did not offer an introduction or a greeting, but simply held out his two cupped hands and parted his thumbs to show me the egg cradled carefully in his palms.

'I found this. Just at the bottom of that cliff-footed ridge, over there to the east, where the elah trees grow.' His wet face was flushed, the blue eyes – deep blue like his mother's – sparkling with excitement and urgency. 'My mother says you know almost everything – she told me you are to be my teacher when I'm old enough. I'm five now – I'll be six in the month of vine pruning, and my mother says I'm to come to you then. But I told Hophra we had to come today, because I want to know what to do with this. I would have climbed up and put it back in the nest, but Hophra wouldn't let me. He said the rock is too slippery in the rain. I think it must be an eagle's egg. It was a very big nest – you could just make out the edge of it.'

'It *is* an eagle's nest,' I said, struggling to retain my composure. I had awaited this day for a long time. Now my head was light with joy and excitement. I took a deep breath, trying to sound calm. 'There is a pair that returns to that ridge every year. Come here, where it's warm, get dry and we'll decide what to do about this egg.'

He stood patiently while Hophra toweled off his rain-slicked hair. He politely accepted a bowl of warmed broth, then we sat by the fire and I read to him from a scroll that gave an account of the ways of eagles. 'Since we can't be sure when this egg was laid, we don't know when it will hatch,' I said. 'Also, it may have been addled in the fall. But since we can't return it to the nest, the best thing you can do is build something like a nest – soft and warm. Then wait. If it does hatch, and you feed it, it will attach itself to you. It will be yours, if you want it.'

'I do!' he said, his face lit with pleasure. But then he frowned. 'I can't take it home. My older brothers, they're not very nice to animals. Especially if they see that it's something I care about. They'll smash it on the stones, just for sport.'

'Then leave it here. You can come every day, if you like, and see how it does.'

'I would like that, very much, if they'll let me.'

'I'm sure they will let you. But I will speak to them, if you think that will help.'

And so it began. Without ceremony, without even an introduction, he became part of my life. Indeed, he became its whole purpose. Every day, I looked forward to the sound of his small, enthusiastic fist knocking on the outer door. I had to discipline myself not to wait for him, staring out the window, watching the path like some lovesick swain. She had named him Schlomo, from the word for peace, *shalom*, but also from the word that in some uses means 'replacement,' because he was the child she hoped would bring consolation after bereavement.

I grew to adore that intense little face, the way his brow would wrinkle before he asked a question. And such questions, from the mouth of a child. 'All streams flow into the sea,' he said. 'Yet the sea is never full. How is that?' Or, 'The sun rises and the sun sets, and glides back to where it rises. How does it make that journey?' These were the questions of a curious intelligence and I did my best to answer them, drawing on scrolls from Mitzrayim and the teaching of astronomers from Ur. But sometimes his face would crease and the question would be so profound that one could hardly credit that it issued from the mind of a small boy. 'Men are born and they die, but the earth remains forever. Why, then, do we set such store on our short lives? Can they matter so much as we think they do?' In such cases, I blundered on as best I could, praying for inspiration, terrified that a weak answer or, worse, a platitude would shake his trust and draw him away from me. But that did not happen. To my joy, he seemed to look forward to our time together as much as I did.

The egg he had rescued hatched – as I knew it would, since I had seen the eaglet in the vision. It was a ball of dandelion fluff with a vociferous call and a tremendous appetite. Schlomo was immensely tender and patient with it, shredding the flesh of river fish, feeding it strand by strand, laughing when he couldn't keep pace with the hatchling's noisy demands. The bird's growth was so rapid it seemed to change appearance every day.

'You know the eagle is called the king of the sky,' I said. 'Why do you think that's so?' We talked about the eagle's keen eyes, and how a king also must be visionary, looking beyond the surface of things; how its speed and strength surpassed other birds, just as a king must hope to surpass his subjects. We talked about its ability to find prey, and how a king also must be a provider for his people.

And then, unexpectedly: 'An eagle is ruthless and takes whatever he wants,' he said. 'Kings do that too.' He ran a finger gently over the eaglet's downy head. It closed its eyes and stretched its neck with pleasure. 'My brother Amnon told me that my father took my mother that way.' [...]

[H]e turned to me and the words came out in a rush. 'I don't think Amnon will be a good king. He hates the ordinary people. He doesn't care about them at all. He's half asleep at the public audiences and he barely ever bothers to go to Father's councils. But Avshalom is always there, when he's allowed to be. I think my father wishes Avshalom were the eldest. Amnon scares you doing what he wants. Avshalom's smarter. He makes you think he likes you, even if he doesn't, not really ...' He stopped abruptly. He must have noticed the pained expression on my face, and misconstrued it. 'Of course, I wouldn't say these things to anyone else. Just to you. I can say anything to you, can't I? Like I do with my mother.'

I needed to tread carefully. 'Has she spoken to you, of who will be king after ... after ...' I found I couldn't bring myself to say the words.

'Just one time. She said that not every king passes his throne to the eldest son.'

'That's true,' I said. 'We don't have a long tradition of kingship, as some other nations do. If your father lives long enough, the time will come when he will decide who will succeed him, and it will need to be someone the people will accept. But that decision could be years off. He's still a vigorous man.'

He tilted his head and looked at me, his eyes widening. I didn't have to spell it out. Even as a child, he could catch an inference. I could see him turning the thought over in his mind.

'It's early to speak of this. Put it out of your mind, for now,' I said. 'For now, you are doing the best thing, soaking up learning and wisdom. If you like, I will speak to the king about letting you go to the minor councils. You never know, he may allow it, young as you are. For now, it's time to practice your reading.' I tapped a finger on the papyrus I'd brought from the palace library. 'Although it isn't the power it was in Ramses' time, Mitzrayim is still an important nation for us. Your father was wise to make peace there. Whoever is king after him will need to keep that peace. Did you know that Mitzrayimites call their writing 'god signs'? They understand that words have power ...' We turned our attention to deciphering the glyphs, and he, delighted and puzzled, threw himself fully into this new challenge.

SELMA

From *The Kiss of Sadaam*

by Michelle McDonald

Selma is an upper-class Iraqi woman, from a liberal family, married to a successful Iraqi diplomat. She has had a privileged life with him but he has recently become a political outcast during President Sadaam Hussein's rise to power. Selma's husband is now in prison. In this scene, she is speaking to a particular woman, a friend who is interviewing her, not to the audience. Selma is telling the story of how she approached Sadaam to request her husband's release from prison.

There is a lot going on underneath this edited piece, even leaving aside the complicated politics of the region. It is based on a true story and the woman Selma is speaking to is Michelle McDonald, who wrote the book after interviewing her and becoming a friend.

The scene Selma describes is tense with sexual menace. She is not used to encountering this, although Sadaam has a reputation and she half expects that this will be an at least confronting meeting. Many years later, with hindsight, she has a dignified reserve. She does not really want to speak of what she had to go through to get her husband freed. Her composure masks deeper feelings about the events she narrates. When she had this meeting she was slightly naïve and fearful, and more than a little enthralled by Sadaam's power. In this present-day scene we need to feel her courage and resilience.

We have included a paragraph from the end of the book in which her personal changes since meeting Sadaam are very clear, but you may wish to end with her defiant response to the driver's question.

I sat there, on the left-hand side of the room, facing him. A man and a woman sat beside me, the others sat on the other side. When we were in the secretary's office my folder had been on the top of the pile. Sadaam leafed through the folders, glancing at each one for what seemed like an eternity but was probably only thirty seconds to a minute. He put my folder on the bottom. My only thought then was, 'I am finished.'

He stood up. He came around and started to shake hands and talk to people. Most people kept sitting, but I stood up. He said, 'Sit down.' I said, 'Sir, I can't sit as long as you are standing – it is improper to sit when I am talking to you.' He smiled and shrugged his shoulders. He asked the people one by one, 'What do you need?' And one said, 'I have lost my son', and another said, 'My neighbours took my house', and another said, 'I haven't seen my son for a year' – things like that. He didn't say anything, just wrote things down, gave them their folders and asked them to leave.

I was left alone in the room with him. I was thirty-two years old and weighed only forty-six kilos; I could not have felt more vulnerable. I felt my heart drop onto the floor. Oh my God – what am I going to say? My mother had said to me, 'Repeat verses from the Koran to help you … When there comes the help of Allah to you, against your enemies …' and I forgot everything – everything. Even if you had asked me my name, I couldn't have answered you. And he went back to his desk and he pointed to a chair and I sat on that chair. There was my silence – I don't know for how long – and I looked down at my hands, clenched in my lap. 'I know why you are here. I know you come for your husband.' He paused. 'He is worthless. He does not deserve to be free.' He spoke quietly but deliberately.

'This is your opinion, your excellency – whatever you say I obey you and I submit to it.'

'Can you believe, a person brings a present to the president and doesn't give it to me?' His voice was hard. What was he saying? And I remembered – my husband ordered a painting as a gift, and when he told the people in the palace that he had brought the president a painting, those people said, 'That's good, we can put it in our office.' And my husband didn't give it to them because he was concerned the president would never receive it. And somehow the opportunity to give it to him hadn't arisen. The pettiness of it took my breath away but I regained my wits and said to Sadaam, 'Your excellency, the present is still in our house. My husband wanted to give it to you himself. We didn't want to give it to a person who wouldn't pass it on to you. It is still there.'

He said, 'Okay, okay … I think your husband is arrogant. He thinks that he knows everything.'

Now I could hear a trace of impatience in his voice. Quickly I said, 'Yes, sir, as you say, sir. But …' I stopped, almost too frightened to say the words. 'Will he be out of prison?'

'You want him to get out of prison?' He laughed.

He stood and came around the desk and I also stood. He grabbed me roughly and started to kiss me and touch me. And he kept touching me, everywhere, intimately – my breasts, my thighs – and he said, 'You have a fine body – keep it, look after it.' He said, 'You are a nice-looking woman.' He didn't say I was beautiful or gorgeous, no, he said you are a nice-looking woman and your body is very fine. My arms were pinned to my side and I could feel his stiff military uniform, his belt, his buttons pressed into me. I felt as stiff as his uniform, tense. I couldn't move away from him, I couldn't respond to his kisses. I could have been a doll, unbending, with wide open eyes that saw nothing. And he continued kissing, his tongue in my mouth, and licking, licking my face, my neck, my breasts – for more than ten minutes.

I had nothing to say to him but the words 'Do you know who I am, sir?' came unthinking from my mouth. He laughed and stopped kissing me for long enough to say, 'Of course, Sadaam Hussein knows every single Iraqi.' Then he kept on kissing and licking and touching. I said, 'Please, I will give myself to you, just get him out of prison.'

He said, 'I wouldn't need permission to have you, if I want you. If you are here or there, if he is in prison or out of prison, whenever I want you I can have you.' Then he released me and I was bleeding … where did I get this blood? From his uniform, a pin, had I crushed my own fingernails into my hand? I was in a daze. If you gave a person heroin, he would not have been as drugged as me. […]

You know he was a handsome man, charismatic, maybe sexy, I don't know. But I was so frightened and … you have an expression in English, 'time stood still'. […]

Then he said to me, 'Okay, we will see. Where do you live?' I told him where I lived and he said, 'You will eat with me tonight.' It was a statement, not a question. I felt my face go cold and my skin prickled and I don't know where my courage came from but I said to Sadaam Hussein, 'I left my two children … sir, I wouldn't have dreamed you would honour me with dinner. I am so sorry, I can't because …' He interrupted: 'Okay, okay, no problem. I'll ask my secretary to take you to your house and now … who brought you?' I told him my sister's husband was waiting outside the palace for me. He picked up the telephone and ordered that my brother-in-law be told to leave and that a car be brought for me.

[As soon as I got in, the driver of the car said] 'You can smoke now.' [I am] certain that he thought that [I] had had sex with Sadaam. […]

[I] said, 'No, thank you, there is no need.' […]

I weep for my homeland, I weep for the life of my sisters, my brother, my mother. I thank God that my father did not live to see the worst excesses of Sadaam Hussein, this once so promising leader, nor the American solution, where our beautiful cities were reduced to battlefields and our people live in poverty and terror. But our culture has lasted for thousands of years. It has been glorious. It will be again.

THE WOMAN

From 'Song of Solomon'
King James Bible

Here we have extracted the woman's voice from this famous poem. These verses are from the 1611 King James version of the Bible, one of the glories of English literature, whatever else one might think of the Bible. The language is Jacobean but eminently playable – it should be relished. Her passion underlies everything she says. She praises her lover, then is disappointed, then finds him again. She (and he, in the verses we have left out) is speaking to the 'daughters of Jerusalem', and in some of the verses here they speak back to her, like a Greek chorus, and question her. But she is always conscious of her lover's presence, at least in her imagination and desire, and that is what you should play.

Let him kiss me with the kisses of his mouth: for thy love is better than wine.

Because of the savour of thy good ointments thy name is as ointment poured forth, therefore do the virgins love thee.

Draw me, we will run after thee: the king hath brought me into his chambers: we will be glad and rejoice in thee, we will remember thy love more than wine: the upright love thee.

I am black, but comely, O ye daughters of Jerusalem, as the tents of Ke-dar, as the curtains of Solomon.

Look not upon me, because I am black, because the sun hath looked upon me: my mother's children were angry with me; they made me the keeper of the vineyards; but mine own vineyard have I not kept.

Tell me, O thou whom my soul loveth, where thou feedest, where thou makest thy flock to rest at noon: for why should I be as one that turneth aside by the flocks of thy companions?

The voice of my beloved! behold, he cometh leaping upon the mountains, skipping upon the hills.

My beloved is like a roe or a young hart: behold, he standeth behind our wall, he looketh forth at the windows, shewing himself through the lattice.

My beloved spake, and said unto me, Rise up, my love, my fair one, and come away.

For, lo, the winter is past, the rain is over and gone;

The flowers appear on the earth; the time of the singing of birds is come, and the voice of the turtle is heard in our land;

The fig tree putteth forth her green figs, and the vines with the tender grape give a good smell. Arise, my love, my fair one, and come away.

O my dove, that art in the clefts of the rock, in the secret places of the stairs, let me see thy countenance, let me hear thy voice; for sweet is thy voice, and thy countenance is comely.

Take us the foxes, the little foxes, that spoil the vines: for our vines have tender grapes.

My beloved is mine, and I am his: he feedeth among the lilies.

Until the day break, and the shadows flee away, turn, my beloved, and be thou like a roe or a young hart upon the mountains of Be-ther.

By night on my bed I sought him whom my soul loveth: I sought him but I found him not.

I will rise now, and go about the city in the streets, and in the broad ways I will seek him whom my soul loveth: I sought him, but I found him not.

The watchmen that go about the city found me: to whom I said, Saw ye him whom my soul loveth?

It was but a little that I passed from them, but I found him whom my soul loveth: I held him, and would not let him go, until I had brought him into my mother's house, and into the chamber of her that conceived me.

I charge you, O ye daughters of Jerusalem, by the roes, and by the hinds of the field, that ye stir not up, nor awake my love, till he please.

I sleep, but my heart waketh: it is the voice of my beloved that knocketh, saying, Open to me, my sister, my dove, my undefiled: for my head is filled with dew, and my locks with the drops of the night.

I have put off my coat; how shall I put it on? I have washed my feet; how shall I defile them?

My beloved put in his hand by the hole of the door, and my bowels were moved for him.

I rose up to open for my beloved; and my hands dropped with myrrh, and my fingers with sweet smelling myrrh, upon the handles of the lock.

I opened to my beloved; but my beloved had withdrawn himself, and was gone: my soul failed when he spake: I sought him, but I could not find him; I called him, but he gave me no answer.

The watchmen that went about the city found me, they smote me, they wounded me; the keepers of the walls took away my veil from me.

I charge you, O daughters of Jerusalem, if ye find my beloved, that ye tell him, that I am sick of [with] love.

What is thy beloved more than another beloved, O thou fairest among women? What is thy beloved more than another beloved, that thou dost so charge us?

My beloved is white and ruddy, the chiefest among ten thousand

His head is as the most fine gold, his locks are bushy, and black as a raven.

His eyes are as the eyes of doves by the rivers of waters, washed with milk, and fitly set.

His cheeks are as a bed of spices, as sweet flowers: his lips like lilies, dropping sweet smelling myrrh.

His hands are as gold rings set with the beryl: his belly is as bright ivory overlaid with sapphires.

His legs are as pillars of marble, set upon sockets of fine gold: his countenance is as Leb-a-non, excellent as the cedars.

His mouth is most sweet: yea, he is altogether lovely. This is my beloved, and this is my friend, O daughters of Jerusalem.

I am my beloved's, and his desire is toward me.

Come, my beloved, let us go forth into the field; let us lodge in the villages.

Let us get up early to the vineyards; let us see if the vine flourish, whether the tender grape appear, and the pomegranates bud forth: there will I give thee my loves.

The mandrakes give a smell, and at our gates are all manner of pleasant fruits, new and old, which I have laid up for thee, O my beloved.

O that thou wert as my brother, that sucked the breasts of my mother! when I should find thee without, I would kiss thee; yea, I should not be despised.

I would lead thee, and bring thee into my mother's house, who would instruct me: I would cause thee to drink of spiced wine of the juice of my pomegranate.

His left hand should me under my head, and his right hand should embrace me.

I charge you, O daughters of Jerusalem, that ye stir not up, nor awake my love, until he please.

Who is this that cometh up from the wilderness, leaning upon her beloved? I raised thee up under the apple tree: there thy mother brought thee forth: there she brought thee forth that bare thee.

Set me as a seal upon thine heart, as a seal upon thine arm: for love is strong as death; jealousy is cruel as the grave: the coals thereof are coals of fire, which hath a most vehement flame.

Many waters cannot quench love, neither can the floods drown it: if a man would give all the substance of his house for love, it would utterly be contemned.

We have a little sister, and she hath no breasts: what shall we do for our sister in the day when she shall be spoken for?

If she be a wall, we will build upon her a palace of silver: and if she be a door, we will inclose her with boards of cedar.

I am a wall, and my breasts are like towers: then was I in his eyes as one that found favour.

Solomon had a vineyard at Baal-ha-mon; he let out the vineyard unto keepers; every one for the fruit thereof was to bring a thousand pieces of silver.

My vineyard, which is mine, is before me: thou, O Solomon, must have a thousand, and those that keep the fruit thereof two hundred.

Thou that dwellest in the gardens, the companions harken to thy voice: cause me to hear it.

Make haste, my beloved, and be thou like a roe or to a young hart upon the mountains of spices.

ME

From Me, Antman and Fleabag
by Gayle Kennedy

The storyteller here is a Wongaibon woman from the desert region of western New South Wales. She is lively and passionate as she describes her experiences travelling around with her bloke Antman and their dog Fleabag. Here, towards the end of the book, she finally gets round to telling us the story of how the three of them first hooked up.

There is a great sense of energy and humour bubbling in her. She has been caught between two worlds, and as a result has, gone wild in the city and then returned home to her people. Now she tells us something very important to her, how she found a kind of resolution between the two worlds. There is real love underneath. She is profoundly moved by what she has found in life. Her journey is from her initial confusion towards accepting her dual identity and feeling at home in her skin.

I'm the first born of Ma and Dad and come into this world a healthy seven and a half pound baby. I stayed that way for the first coupla years of me life, living with Ma and Dad out in the desert country.

Then Ma went to hospital to have my brother. She left me laughing, happy and healthy. Five days later she returned to me lying in a cot, barely able to breathe. She tried to make me stand. I collapsed. She took me in her arms and ran the five miles into town. That was the beginning of me nightmare. I was real sick. The doctors flew me to hospital for children in the city and …

I stayed there for a few years. When I was well enough, I was sent to a convalescent home to learn to walk again, to be rehabilitated. For the next three years, from the onset of the illness to me eventual reunion with me family, I did not once see another blackfulla, let alone even see another Aboriginal face.

When you're a little fulla you see your reflection in those around you. And all the faces that surrounded me were white. They wore stiff, starched uniforms, everything was clean, antiseptic, and everything was ordered. I lived in a safe, clean, little white world.

Then came the day that me and Ma and Dad will never forgit. It started out like any other day – up early, bathed, fed. The only thing different I was dressed in a brand new pinafore, new top, shoes, socks and me hair was tied in ribbons. I was thinkin I was going for a day out with Linda the cook. Anyway, I was excited about the new clothes. I felt like a princess. Then I was told I was going to meet some special people and they were taking me on a long journey.

'But they'll bring me home, won't they?' I said.

They were evasive. 'Maybe one day. For a visit.'

'Are they taking me away forever and ever? They can't do that, can they?'

I saw tears in the nursing sister's eyes. I was confused and started to feel frightened.

Then I was taken to the visitors' room where before me stood two aliens from another world. It was Ma and Dad.

'This is your mummy and daddy,' said the sister as she passed me to the strange dark lady.

I remember screamin. 'She's not Mummy, he's not Daddy. They're black.'

Tears streamed down their faces. I reckon it woulda hurt em real bad. I was handed over to these two dark-skinned and cryin strangers, screamin in terror. No one gave me a chance to git ta know these people. After all those years they just handed me to em. Just like that.

Ma and Dad carried me, still screaming, into a bustling, noisy, crowded railway station, desperately tryin to ignore the suspicious stares of the strangers around em. All their soothing and strokin did no good. I just kept right on cryin, even when we got into the carriage at Central. Suddenly, the train began to move and soon we were passin through suburbs and then countryside. I started gittin curious.

'Where are we going? Is that a real cow? Are you really my mummy and daddy?'

'We're goin home now, me baby', said the dark-skinned lady.

Now that I wasn't struggling, she seemed so soft. Her eyes were big and brown but full of tears.

'You mean back to the ward?'

'No, baby girl, back to your real home. You got a baby brother and sister. They're called Buddy and Lulla. Home to your grandma and grandpa.'

I started to relax. Daddy was makin funny faces at me and pointing out the animals. The trip seemed to take forever, but this kind and gentle woman held me all the way. When I became sleepy, I nestled my head in her breasts, and her blouse was damp from both our tears. I went to sleep.

The next morning, the train pulled up at a small railway station, smack dab in the middle of a vast red desert. There were no big trees, just little saltbush ones. A radio was blarin from the station office, breakin the eerie silence as we stepped off the train.

I was used to the big houses and leafy surrounds of the North Shore. These people I had started to trust really were aliens. They had taken me to Mars.

Daddy took me from Mum and hoisted me on his shoulders. We started walking across the vast expanse of red earth and strange little trees. We saw some emus and a kangaroo. A big yellow lizard ran in front of us. It was so hot. We seemed to walk for miles and then I could hear the sound of laughter. Someone was strumming a guitar and singin. We walked into a clearin, where in a circle were huts made from scrap, tents and a coupla caravans. There were dogs and kids everywhere and people all the same colour as the people who had brought me here.

It sure did come as a surprise when I finally looked into a mirror and realised I was the same colour as them. [...]

For a long time I lived in two worlds. One white, one black, and never really fitting into either. I went home often for Christmas, Easter, but family reminiscences left me out. I hadn't been there. Me brothers and sisters didn't seem to understand that I never wanted to be away when I was a kid.

I hardly knew the family, let alone my culture. All those years I drifted from one world to another, part of me missing.

I drank too much, probably, and could never bear to be in a job longer than six months. Anyone who tried to get too close was pushed away. It was just too hard. It was funny too. Cos even when I was in the arms of other fullas, some that I even really liked, my soul felt lonely. My skin felt lonely.

Then Antman came along. [...]

It aint that he was the best lookin fulla I ever saw, it was just that it felt like I was seein the lights of home for the first time. Next thing ya know, he's lookin right back at me while he's singin [Koorioke in the pub] and when he finishes he comes straight over and introduces himself. That was it. I went home with him that night. We talked all night bout all kinds of things.

Turns out Antman had been crook when he was little fulla too. Spent a long time away from his family, just like me. We loved the same things – readin books, listenin to music, dogs, Slim Dusty, bein outside.

And before too long, we loved each other. Two days later he drove round to the house I'd been livin in and I packed a suitcase, grabbed my guitar and we ain't been apart since.

It wasn't easy the first year. We was both used to bein on our own, doin what we pleased. We kept pullin each other in different directions.

One night, after I had too much to drink, we had a terrible fight. The next day I was feelin sorry, feelin shame, askin him to forgive me.

He looked at me and said, 'I bet you've done this a thousand times. Always asking for forgiveness, always thinking it's your fault. You don't think you're worthy of love. You don't know yourself. I gotta take you home, girl. Back to your people, your country. It won't be easy but you'll never find peace until you stop runnin.'

For the first time I listened to what someone else had to say. Finally someone was makin sense.

The next week we packed up the car and he took me back to the red dirt. Back to family, country, culture.

We lived for the next coupla a years with my mob. We listened to the stories of our old people, learn our language. I discovered my blackness. It wasn't easy. Strangely enough, while I was feeling sorry for myself because of my sickness and enforced separation, turns out the rest of the kids thought I had lived a privileged life.

[After a while] me and Antman reckoned it was time to go back to the city for a spell. Just before we were about to leave one of me sisters come by with a little bundle of pure white stuff. Lulla reckoned they couldn't find im a home cos he had a gammy leg from birth. She reckoned we needed him and he needed us. Antman took im from her and give im a big cuddle and said,

'Welcome home, ya little fleabag.'

And that was that. The next day he sat in the front seat between the two of us and he's been ridin there ever since. He's the greatest little mutt ever. He's cheeky and smart and he don't worry bout his gammy leg, just runs with the rest of the pack. All the blackfullas love im ta bits, specially the old fullas who fuss over im and tell us off if they reckon we aint lookin after im. Lulla was right, we sure did need that little fulla. Still do.

Fleabag's our kid. Antman can't have kids on account he had ta have chemotherapy when he was young and my sickness meant I couldn't have any either. I suppose we three was meant to hook up.

A few months after we got Flea, we was all lyin in bed. It was early morning, just before the sun come up. Antman was asleep with his arm across my belly and Fleabag's usin my leg for a pillow.

I suddenly felt all the loneliness leave me, finally makin room for all the good things in life, like family, laughin, travellin and, best of all, love.

Suddenly I felt all together. There was no more lonely soul, no more lonely skin.

DAVID

From 'See You Again Yesterday' in *Me Talk Pretty One Day*

by David Sedaris

In this piece David talks to the audience with a comic flair. This is an edited extract from the original essay. The titles of the essay and the book are references to his pathetic attempts to learn French and in the extract he recounts a special time in his life: when he fell in love, and then moved to France, with Hugh. He performs this with lightness and wit, and a bit of mock self-deprecation, that is very funny. Underneath the stylish presentation there is a lot of love for Hugh.

I have never been one of those Americans who pepper their conversation with French phrases and entertain guests with wheels of brie. For me, France was never a specific, premeditated destination. I wound up in Normandy the same way my mother wound up in North Carolina: you meet a guy, relinquish a tiny bit of control, and the next thing you know, you're eating a different part of the pig.

I met Hugh through a mutual friend. She and I were painting an apartment, and he offered the use of his twelve-foot ladder. Owning a twelve-foot ladder in New York is a probable sign of success, as it means you most likely have enough room to store one. At the time, Hugh was living in a loft on Canal Street, a former chocolate factory where the walk-in coolers had been turned into bedrooms. I arrived at his place on a Friday night and noticed the pie baking in the oven. While the rest of Manhattan was out on the town, he'd stayed home to peel apples and listen to country music.

Like me, Hugh was single, which came as no great surprise, considering that he spent his leisure time rolling out dough and crying to George Jones albums. I had just moved to New York and was wondering if I was going to be alone for the rest of my life. Part of the problem was that, according to several reliable sources, I tended to exhaust people. Another part of the problem had to do with my long list of standards. Potential boyfriends could not smoke Merit cigarettes, own or wear a pair of cowboy boots, or eat anything labelled *lite* or *heart smart*. Speech was important, and disqualifying phrases included 'I can't find my nipple ring' and 'This one here was my *first* tattoo.' [...]

Hugh had moved to New York after spending six years in France. I asked a few questions, rightly sensing that he probably wouldn't offer anything unless provoked. There was, he said, a house in Normandy. This was most likely followed by a qualifier, something pivotal like 'but it's a dump'. He probably described it in detail, but by that point I was only half listening. Instead, I'd begun to imagine my life in a foreign country, some faraway land where, if things went wrong, I could always blame someone else, saying I'd never wanted to live there in the first place. [...]

'Built around 1780 ... a two hour train ride from Paris ... the neighbour keeps his horses in my backyard ... pies made with apples from my own trees ...'

I caught the highlights of Hugh's broadcast and understood that my first goal was to make him my boyfriend, to trick or blackmail him into making some sort of commitment. I know it sounds calculating, but if you're not cute, you might as well be clever.

In order to get the things I want, it helps me to pretend I'm a figure in a daytime drama, a schemer. Soap opera characters make emphatic pronouncements. They ball up their fists and state their goals out loud. 'I *will* destroy Buchanan Enterprises,' they say. 'Phoebe Wallingford *will* pay for what she's done to our family.' Walking home with the back half of the twelve-foot ladder, I turned to look in the direction of Hugh's loft. 'You *will* be mine,' I commanded.

Nine months after I borrowed the ladder, Hugh left the chocolate factory and we moved in together. As was his habit, he planned to spend the month of August in Normandy, visiting friends and working on his house. I'd planned to join him, but that first year, when the time came to buy my ticket, I chickened out, realizing that I was afraid of France. My fear had nothing to do with the actual French people. What scared me was the idea of French people I'd gotten from movies and situation comedies. When someone makes a spectacular ass of himself, it's always in a French restaurant, never a Japanese or Italian one. The French are the people who slap one another with gloves and wear scarves to cover their engorged hickies. My understanding was that, no matter how hard we tried, the French would never like us, and that's confusing to an American raised to believe that the citizens of Europe should be grateful for all the wonderful things we've done. Things like movies that stereotype the people of France as boors and petty snobs, and little remarks such as 'We saved your ass in World War II.' Every day we're told that we live in the greatest country on earth. And it's always stated as an undeniable fact: Leos are born between July 23 and August 22, fitted queen-size sheets measure sixty by eighty inches, and America is the greatest country on earth. Having grown up with this in our ears, it's startling to realize that other countries have nationalistic slogans of their own, none of which are 'We're number two!'

The French have decided to ignore our self-proclaimed superiority, and this is translated as arrogance. To my knowledge, they've never said that they're better than us; they've just never said that we're the best. Big deal. There are plenty of places on earth where visiting Americans are greeted with great enthusiasm. Unfortunately, these places tend to lack anything you'd really want to buy. And that, to me, is the only reason to leave home in the first place – to buy things. Hugh bought me great gifts the summer I stayed home and he went off to France. He's not really much of a shopper, so I figured that if he managed to find these things, they must have been right out in the open where anyone could have spotted them. As far as I was concerned, the French could be cold or even openly hostile. They could burn my flag or pelt me with stones, but if there were taxidermied kittens to be had, then I would go and bring them back to this, the greatest country on earth.

There was the shopping, and then there was the smoking. Hugh returned from his trip, and days later I still sounded like a Red Chinese asking questions about the democratic hinterlands. 'And you actually saw people smoking in restaurants? Really! And offices, too? Oh, tell me again about the ashtrays in hospital waiting rooms, and don't leave anything out.'

When the cranes arrived to build a twelve-story hotel right outside our bedroom window, Hugh and I decided to leave New York for a year or two, just until our resentment died down a little. I'm determined to learn as much French as possible, so we'll take an apartment in Paris, where there are posters and headlines and any number of words waiting to be captured and transcribed onto index cards, where a person can comfortably smoke while making a spectacular ass of himself, and where, when frustrated, I can lie, saying I never wanted to come here in the first place.

OVID

From *An Imaginary Life* by David Malouf

The speaker here is an old man and the story is of his death. The writer has imagined a life for Ovid, who exiled himself from his aristocratic rural childhood (including, in the book, his glimpses of a wolf-boy child whom only he can see) and went to imperial Rome, where he became a great poet, before being exiled again to the far reaches of the Empire because he displeased the Emperor Augustus.

This is the final passage of the novel. The context is that during his second exile Ovid meets an actual 'wolf-boy' – a wild Child as remote from Roman civilisation as it is possible to be – and befriends him, first as his teacher and then as his pupil. Forced to flee the rough settlement where they have been living, they cross a river and move further away into the wild eastern steppes, living precariously off the land.

You can't play all this, of course, in this short piece, but it is implied in what Ovid says here, lying in the grass in the spot that will be his last. He is speaking to the audience but his attention is on the Child moving off into the light. The action is that, after all their unlikely bonding, Ovid is coming to terms with his death and is joyfully letting his wild young friend go.

The poetry in the writing suggests the scene's spirituality: that in some sense Ovid, a civilised urban poet, is returning to his childhood and to the earth, and that his spirit has somehow become merged with the spirit of the Child.

And so we come to it, the place. I have taken my last step, though he does not know it yet, as he moves away as usual to forage for our evening meal. From here I ascend, or lower myself, grain by grain, into the hands of the gods. It is the place I dreamed of so often, back there in Tomis, but could never find in all my wanderings in sleep – the point on the earth's surface where I disappear.

It is not at all as I had imagined. There are no wolves. It is clear sunlight, at the end of a day like each of the others we have spent out here, a fine warm spring day with larks in the air, and insects shrilling under our feet. The Child is here. I watch him moving away along the edge of a stream, stooping, kneeling, starting off again with his spring-heeled gait as he gathers snails amongst the weeds.

Strange to look back on the enormous landscape we have struggled across all these weeks, across the sea, across my life in Rome, across my childhood, to observe how clearly the footprints lead to this place and no other. They shine in my head, all those steps. I can, in my mind, follow them back, feeling myself with each step restored, diminished, till I come to the ground of my earliest memories again, and am standing in the checkered light of olives at the very edge of our farm, with wings glittering beyond the low stone wall and a goatherd dozing against one of the olives, his rough head tilted back and all the throat exposed, as if he had been dozing like that, just as I last remember him, for nearly sixty years. One of the goats, which is black, has just jerked up on to its hind legs to munch at a vine shoot. It is spring. It is summer. I am three years old. I am sixty.

The Child is there.

He turns for a moment to gaze at me across his shoulder, which is touched with sunlight, then stoops to gather another snail from the edge of the stream. He rises and goes on. The stream shakes out its light around his ankles as he wades deeper, then climbs on to a smooth stone and balances for a moment in the sun, leaps, leaps again, then wanders upstream on the other bank, which is gravel, every pebble of it, white, black, gray, picked out and glittering in the late sunlight as in a mosaic, where he pauses, gathers one, two, four snails, and with the stream rippling as he steps in and out of it, walks on, kicking at the gravel with his toes and lost for a moment in his own childlike pleasure at being free.

I might call to him. I have the voice for that. But do not. To call him back might be to miss the fullness of this moment as it is about to be revealed, and I want so much, at the very end here, to be open to all that it holds for me.

The fullness is in the Child's moving away from me, in his stepping so lightly, so joyfully, naked, into his own distance at last as he fades in and out of the dazzle of light off the water and stoops to gather – what? Pebbles? Is that what his eye is attracted by now, the grayest, most delicately veined of them? Or has he already forgotten all purpose, moving simply for the joy of it, wading deeper into the light and letting them fall from his hands, the living and edible snails that are no longer necessary to my life and may be left now to return to their own, the useless pebbles that where they strike the ground suddenly flare up as butterflies, whose bright wings rainbow the stream.

He is walking on the water's light. And as I watch, he takes the first step off it, moving slowly away now into the deepest distance, above the earth, above the water, on air.

It is summer. It is spring. I am unmeasurably, unbearably happy. I am three years old. I am sixty. I am six.

I am there.

'I Have Never Seen You' by Jyoti Lanjewar

This is a famous poem by the Marathi Dalit writer Jyoti Lanjewar. It is short, but we offer it for what you can do with it, as it is very powerful and beautiful. The Dalit are the outcast 'Untouchables' in the hierarchical Indian caste system, and Lanjewar here pays tribute to the work of Dalit women and their resilience in raising their children in the face of poverty and extreme hardship.

'Ambedkar', 'Bhim' and 'Baba' all refer to Dr Bhimrao Ramji Ambedkar, a social reformer who campaigned for Dalit rights and was an architect of the Indian Constitution. 'Diksha Bhoomi' is a sacred monument that commemorates his conversion to Buddhism. An Ilkali brocaded sari and gold jewellery would only have been worn by women of high caste. These details can't be easily dramatised in a monologue, but they should inform the attitude of the character you create.

The speaker is an Indian Dalit woman but you will have to find a more specific character for her. Perhaps she is young and angry; perhaps she is older. Certainly she is full of respect and admiration for the strength of the women she is talking to. The details of scenes she describes need to be created and relished. Perhaps she is thinking of her mother or grandmother, but certainly she is seeing these women on stage, and can indicate that in her playing of the poem. Seeing them is the irony of the title, and the point of the whole poem, so you should play that.

I have never seen you
In a brocaded new
Nine-yard *Ilkali* sari
With a gold necklace around your neck
Or gold bangles worn on your hands
Not even rubber sandals on your feet

Burning your soles in the scorching heat
Bundling the tender one of your womb and
Hanging the bundle on the acacia tree
Working with the road construction workers
Carrying barrels of tar
I have seen you.

Your feet bound in rags
Planting a sweaty kiss on the naked child
Coming tottering towards you
Bearing the hunger knotting your entrails
And lips parched for water
Working to build a dam on the lake
On daily wages
Slaving hard
I have seen you

Deluge of tears in your eyes
Eternal summer heat in your life
When the burning sun got off your head
Picking cotton
Keeping it in your sari fold
Pushing behind the plough
Building the future of your children
I have seen you

In crowded streets balancing
The basket load on your head
Wrapping your tattered sari around your body
To guard your honour
Raising your sandal at anyone leering at you
I have seen you.

For a dream of four mud plastered walls
Your feet heavy with pregnancy
Carefully stepping on the scaffolding

Of skyscrapers
Carrying on your head
Scuttles of wet cement
I have seen you

In the late evenings
Untying your sari for coins
To buy oil and salt for cooking
Placing a five paise coin
On your little one's hand
And saying …
'Eat whatever goodies you want
But go to school'
Lifting the little bundle from the cradle
Tenderly holding it to your breast
And saying…
'At least, you study, become like Ambedkar,
And relieve me of this basket load.'
I have seen you

Dragging your feet to your house
Skeletal body … the heat of life
Debts to the moneylender … a ploughshare
Half fed from sunset to dawn
Still refusing to accept charity
Retaining your self-respect
I have seen you

Marching ahead in the Long March
Shouting 'Change the name'
Braving the police batons
Going to jail with head held high
Seeing your only son
Falling martyr to police bullets
Consoling him …
'You died for Bhim, your life now has its meaning.'

Telling the police officer defiantly …
'If I had two, three or four more sons, how good it would have been,
They would have fought as well.'
I have seen you.

On your death bed in the hospital
Donating the money you earned rag-picking
To the Diksha Bhoomi
Gathering the last moments of life
And reiterating…
'All of you live in unity
Build a memorial
Fight in the name of Baba.'
And with your dying breath saying
'Jai Bhim'
I have seen you.

I have never seen you
In a brocaded new
Nine-yard *Ilkali* sari

SOURCES

Beckett, M. (1979). *Molloy* (first pub. in English 1955). Picador, pp. 64–69. Copyright © Samuel Beckett. Extract reprinted by permission of Faber & Faber.

Brontë, C. (2012). *Jane Eyre* (first pub. 1847). Penguin, pp.488–491.

Brooks, G. (2015). *The Secret Chord*. Hachette Australia, pp. 278–289. Copyright © Geraldine Brooks. Extract reprinted by permission of Hachette Australia.

Carver, R. (1996). 'Mr Coffee and Mr Fixit', in *What We Talk About When We Talk About Love*, London: Panther, pp. 14–17. Copyright © Raymond Carver. Extract reprinted by permission of The Random House Group Limited.

Defoe, D. (1965). *Moll Flanders* (first pub. 1722). New York: Harper & Row, pp. 192–195.

Dickens, C. (1860). *Great Expectations.* Chapter 29.

Eugenides, J. (2002). *Middlesex*. London: HarperCollins, pp. 434–439. Copyright © Jeffrey Eugenides. Extract reprinted by permission of HarperCollins Publishers Ltd.

Ferrante, E. (2013). *My Brilliant Friend*. Melbourne: Text Publishing, pp. 311–331. Copyright © Elena Ferrante. First published by Europa Editions. Extract reprinted by permission of The Text Publishing Co. Australia, Melbourne.

Gleitzman, M. (2005). *Once*. Penguin, pp. 1–8. Copyright © 2005 Morris Gleitzman. Extract reprinted by permission of Penguin Random House Australia.

Høeg, P. (1994). *Miss Smilla's Feeling for Snow*. London: Harvill Press, pp. 10–13. Copyright © Peter Høeg. Extract reprinted by permission of The Random House Group Limited.

Jerome, J. K. (1993). *Three Men in a Boat* (first published 1889). Hertfordshire: Wordsworth Editions Limited, pp. 5–7.

Jolley, E. (1983). 'The Shed', in *Woman in a Lampshade*. Penguin, pp. 201–207. Copyright © The Estate of Elizabeth Jolley. Extract reprinted by permission of the author's estate, c/- Jenny Darling & Associates.

Joyce, J. (1968). *Ulysses* (first pub. 1922). Penguin, pp. 697–704.

July, M. (2007). *no one belongs here more than you*. Melbourne: Text Publishing, pp. 53–56. Copyright © Miranda July. Extract reprinted by permission of The Wylie Agency (UK) Limited.

Kafka, F. (2005). 'Children on a Country Road', in Nahum N. Glatzer (ed.) *The Complete Short Stories of Franz Kafka*. London: Random House, pp. 379–382.

Kennedy, G. (2008). *Me, Antman and Fleabag*. Brisbane, UQP, pp. 92–102. Copyright © Gayle Kennedy. Extract reprinted by permission of UQP.

King James Bible (first published 1611), 'Song of Solomon', Verses 1:2–6; 2:8–17; 3:1–5; 5:2–16; 7:10–13; 8:1–14.

Lanjewar, J. (2016). 'I Have Never Seen You', in Catriona Mitchell (ed.), *Walking Towards Ourselves: Indian Women Tell Their Stories,* Uttar Pradesh: HarperCollins, pp. 230–234. Copyright © Jyoti Lanjewar. Extract reprinted by permission of C. S. Lakshmi and Sharmila Sontakke.

Leane, J. (2011). *Purple Threads*. Brisbane: UQP, pp. 110–124. Copyright © Jeanine Leane. Extract reprinted by permission of UQP.

Leckie, A. (2013). *Ancillary Justice*. London: Orbit (Little, Brown), pp. 1–8. Copyright © Ann Leckie. Extract reprinted by permission of the rights holder.

Malouf, D. (1980). *An Imaginary Life*. Sydney: Picador, pp. 150–152. Copyright © David Malouf. First published by Chatto & Windus. Extract reprinted by permission of The Random House Group Limited.

Marsden, J. (1994). *The Dead of the Night*. Sydney: Pan Macmillan, pp. 150–156. Copyright © JLM Pty Ltd. Extract reprinted by permission of Pan Macmillan Australia Pty Ltd.

McDonald, M. (2009). *The Kiss of Sadaam*. Brisbane: UQP, pp. 164–169, 243. Copyright © Michelle McDonald. Extract reprinted by permission of UQP.

Munro, A. (2013). 'Amundsen', in *Dear Life*. London: Random House, pp. 58–63. Copyright © Alice Munro. Extract reprinted by permission of The Random House Group Limited.

Plath, S. (1966). *The Bell Jar*. London: Faber and Faber, pp. 127–133. Copyright © Estate of Sylvia Plath. Extract reprinted by permission of Faber & Faber.

Powers, K. (2013). *The Yellow Birds*. Sceptre (Hodder & Stoughton), pp. 205–210. Copyright © Kevin Powers. Extract reprinted by permission of the author c/o Rogers, Coleridge & White Ltd.

Pung, A. (2006). *Unpolished Gem*. Melbourne: Black Inc, pp. 219–232. Copyright © Alice Pung. Extract reprinted by permission of Black Inc.

Sedaris, D. (2002). *Me Talk Pretty One Day*. London: Abacus, pp. 153–165. Copyright © David Sedaris. Extract reprinted by permission of Abner Stein.

Silvey, C. (2009). *Jasper Jones*. Crows Nest: Allen & Unwin, pp. 48–52. Copyright © Craig Silvey. Extract reproduced with permission of Allen & Unwin Pty Ltd.

Twain, M. (1906). *Eve's Diary: Translated from the Original*. London: Harper and Brothers, pp. 3–25.

RELATED TITLES FROM CURRENCY PRESS:

Jasper Jones

Kate Mulvany (adapted from the novel by Craig Silvey)

This theatrical adaptation is wise and beautiful – it features a cast of finely drawn teenagers and grown-ups, all searching for their own kind of truth. A coming-of-age story, *Jasper Jones* interweaves the lives of complex individuals all struggling to find happiness among the buried secrets of a small rural community.

978-1-76062-004-2, also available as a digital edition.

The School Drama Book

Robyn Ewing AM & John Nicholas Saunders

School Drama is a professional learning program for primary school teachers, which focuses on the power of using drama and literature to improve English and literacy in young learners. It was developed by the Sydney Theatre Company (STC) in partnership with The University of Sydney. This book is a comprehensive School Drama resource.

978-1-92500-534-9, also available as a digital edition.

Dramawise Reimagined

Brad Haseman & John O'Toole

This is a new edition of the seminal text *Dramawise*. First published in 1987, *Dramawise* changed the way drama was taught. In this edition, the authors have updated the theory to include more modern theatre practice and exercises that reference more recent Australian work.

978-1-92500-589-9, also available as a digital edition.

Belonging: Australian Drama in the 20th Century

John McCallum

This new history explores the relationship between twentieth-century Australian drama and a developing concept of nation. The book focuses on the creative tension sparked by the duelling impulses of nationalism and cosmopolitanism. This book examines the influence of European high culture and popular theatrical forms on Australian drama, the ambivalence (between affection and aggression) of much Australian humour, and the interaction between the personal and the political in drama.

978-0-86819-658-9, also available as a digital edition.

SEE OUR WEBSITE FOR MORE TITLES: WWW.CURRENCY.COM.AU